FATHER CRY

CRY

HEALING YOUR HEART *and the* HEARTS
OF THOSE YOU LOVE

═══

BILLY WILSON

Chosen
a division of Baker Publishing Group
Minneapolis, Minnesota

© 2012 by William M. Wilson

Published by Chosen Books
11400 Hampshire Avenue South
Bloomington, Minnesota 55438
www.chosenbooks.com

Chosen Books is a division of
Baker Publishing Group, Grand Rapids, Michigan

Printed in the United States of America

Library of Congress Cataloging-in-Publication Data is available for this title.

ISBN 978-0-8007-9538-2 (pbk.)

Cover design by Gearbox

12   13   14   15   16   17   18   7   6   5   4   3   2   1

"In *Father Cry* Billy Wilson touches the heart and soul of a deep need. Read this book with your heart opened! As you do, I hope each young person can hear the heart of leaders like Billy (and me, as well) who truly and deeply care about you!"

Jack W. Hayford, chancellor, The King's University

"*Father Cry* serves as a prophetic and reconciliatory prescription for a generation seeking authentic relationships with spiritual fathers and mothers. Billy Wilson proposes a relationship—rather than imposing a structure—that will heal this generation so God can raise the next."

The Rev. Samuel Rodriguez, president, National Hispanic Christian Leadership Conference

"Read it and reap! This would be my counsel for any parent, pastor or church leader. The cry for spiritual mentors is deafening all around the world. Dr. Wilson shares biblical foundations for effective discipleship along with personal vulnerability and practical strategies. You'll reap from Dr. Wilson's insights and encouragement and the Spirit's prompting."

Josh McDowell, Josh McDowell Ministries

"Billy Wilson gives us the biblical basis for spiritual adoption and appropriate mentoring, sharing that even one's pain can be the platform for present and future ministry. A very moving, practical book."

Tom Phillips, vice president of crusades, Billy Graham Evangelistic Association

"'Hurting people will identify with those who know pain.' With these few words, Dr. Wilson speaks with vulnerability and biblical insight to every parent, pastor and church who longs to pass along a vibrant, Christ-centered faith to the next generations. Drawing upon his Spirit-empowered heritage, Dr. Wilson provides practical strategies for any Christ-follower from any tradition."

Dr. David Ferguson, executive director, Great Commandment Network

"Every child on this planet, from the jungle to the suburbs, from the inner city to the farm, needs a father, a family and a future. Billy Wilson, with prophetic passion and precision, challenges the church to hear the Father's cry and become the Body of Christ Himself, His hands and His feet."

Dr. Jay Strack, president and founder, Student Leadership University

"Billy Wilson asks a critical question for our time: 'Are we willing to reduce relational distance in our churches and in our families?' From his Spirit-empowered roots, he plants fruitful personal insights that are helpful to all Christians needing a refreshing encounter with the love of God the Father."

Mark Brister, Ph.D.; president, Mark Brister Ministries, www.markbristerministries.org

"All of us have been touched by the Father cry reality. We live in a society of 'I am too busy,' at the expense of loved ones who may suffer emotionally for a lifetime, never reaching their God-given potential. A must-read for every parent, pastor and son/daughter."

Pastor Danny de Leon, senior pastor, Templo Calvario Church,
Santa Ana, California

"From a perspective of personal experience and powerful Holy Spirit inspiration, Billy Wilson has sounded an alarm in *Father Cry* that is resonating around the world. In both inspirational and practical ways, he sheds light on the need for spiritual parents to pass the baton of faith to the next generation."

Alton Garrison, assistant general superintendent,
General Council of the Assemblies of God

"There is a desperate need for mentoring the next generation to fulfill their God-given mandate. This book will serve all in the Body of Christ to bring healing while empowering them; to bring freedom while restoring them; to encourage them to reach greater levels in Christ."

Dr. Claudio Freidzon, founding pastor, Iglesia Rey de Reyes,
Buenos Aires, Argentina

"*Father Cry* will touch the hearts of readers regardless of their age. This is a must-read book for the far too many people who have not known the love of a father or mother. Through reading this book, they will be able to cry out 'Abba Father' as they experience His unfathomable love."

Graham Lacey, author, speaker, Kingdom consultant,
London, England

"You will be deeply touched by the words of Billy Wilson as he shares how he cried out with great agony of soul to his earthly father during his formative years. You will rejoice in the way his story ends and give God thanks for Billy's clear call for us to cry out to our heavenly Father."

Paul Cedar, chairman, Mission America Coalition

"The need for spiritual parents and intergenerational mentoring has never been greater. *Father Cry* is a much-needed light of truth that shines on the need for spiritual parents to pour into the lives of hurting young people all over the world. Billy does an excellent job of sharing this truth."

Rob Hoskins, president, OneHope

I would like to dedicate *Father Cry* to the millions of hurting young people around the world who feel abandoned and orphaned by older generations. May this book be used of God to empower you for greatness as God heals your heart and connects you to the spiritual fathers and mothers you need.

Contents

Foreword

In my many years of ministry to next-generation audiences, I have observed firsthand the father cry that Billy Wilson powerfully articulates. Billy and I have joined together in ministry venues, such as the Azusa Street Centennial and the Empowered21 Global Congress, where multiple thousands of youth have voiced a heart cry for Holy Spirit empowerment along with a desperate need for the affirmation of a parent generation. In these settings God has clearly revealed that we are living in the days of a prophetic fulfillment of Malachi's words: "He will turn the hearts of the parents to their children, and the hearts of the children to their parents" (Malachi 4:6). Sharing not only scriptural and statistical insights but his own experiences, Billy opens his heart to you from an intensely personal perspective that brings the Father's message to life for all ages. God's message of love transcends every generation.

When Jesus said, "Love each other" (John 15:12), He used the Greek word for *love* that means "to nurture." Think of a mother and her child: Her love is constant and her greatest desire for her child is that he or she should thrive. God's greatest desire for the Church is that we not only thrive but that we help others grow and develop a personal, loving relationship with Him. Some might say, "But isn't that the kind of love people should get somewhere else, like at home?" No. Beneath the facades, some in your life from the younger generation desperately need to be nurtured. They will be influenced most by those who make them feel best about themselves. One leader writes,

> Many people are very close to my heart because they believed in me when I didn't believe in myself. They listened to me without condemnation and loved me unconditionally, even when I wasn't very lovable. Without them, I wouldn't have possessed the hope I needed to keep pursuing my dream.

Rather than merely being an authority figure, you can become an Elijah or a Paul in the life of a young person needing a cheerleader, not a critic. As Billy sheds light on the need for spiritual parents to pass the baton of faith to the next generation, he challenges us to realize that the mantle of power and anointing must be transferred during this critical "passing zone" of time. You can be one God calls to nurture Elishas or Timothys in a way they will welcome you to speak into their lives—and they will listen. Goethe said, "Correction does much, but encouragement does much more." As chapter 3 clearly reveals, a Naomi also needs a Ruth, a spiritual daughter (or son) who will embrace her encouragement and follow through with her instructions. The results of these intergenerational connections will bring great fruitfulness and the fulfillment of destiny and legacy for the Church, replacing the present father cry with the message of the Messiah.

Father Cry also offers a plan for intervention as Billy answers the question, "What does this mean for my local church?" You can move beyond discussion to engaging possible ways the cry for spiritual parents can be met. This is not something merely proposed but illustrated through direct experience with multiple generations. The book offers a paradigm for an intergenerational retreat model, explaining both positive and challenging discoveries. You will gain practical knowledge along with inspirational motivation as you read the stories of young people crying out and the enthusiasm of older spiritual parents responding.

Dr. Billy Wilson has a multigenerational vision. He opens vistas beyond mentoring to see the Father's plan for spiritual adoption. As he so vividly states, "The Father's arms are open wide. His love is stronger than death. He knows your pain. He sees your struggle, and He still wants you! You were born to be His child, and He delights to be your Father. When no one else responds, and the people around you seem deafened by their own selfishness, Abba Father has not turned away. Lift your voice to Him. He will respond to your father cry!" Cultivated from years of experience and powerful biblical insight, *Father Cry* is a must-read for parents, leaders and students.

Jentezen Franklin
Senior Pastor, Free Chapel Worship Center,
Gainesville, Florida, and Irvine, California;
Host of the internationally televised program
Kingdom Connection

Acknowledgments

Father Cry would not have become a reality without my earthly father, Marion Alva Wilson. The story of God's amazing grace in his life and death forms the bedrock in which this book is anchored. In my personal opinion, he embodied everything a spiritual father should possess, and that is why he was able to impact so many sons and daughters in the faith. Alva was a great man because he was great in loving others. I love you, Dad!

I also honor my mother, Joyce Wilson, and my two sisters, Donna and Marqueta. Our journey through pain and healing has been miraculous. We have shared the tears and laughter you will read about in this book. Mom has been faithful to us through thick and thin; her love at critical moments has made an eternal difference for our whole family.

There are two other special fathers I want to recognize; they are committed Christians and great dads. Ashley Wilson is my son. He lives in Lexington, Kentucky, with his wife, Jamie, and their three children, Anna, Aaron and Amelia. He pastors a new church plant and serves his family well. Shaun Morton is my son-in-law. Shaun, along with my daughter, Sara, and their two children, Abigail and Samuel, live in Paraguay in South America, where they lead a home for abandoned children, a community school and an outreach. Shaun is a great dad. Sara and Shaun's amazing care for the broken children of Paraguay humbles and challenges me to make love more practical.

My wife, Lisa, is the greatest woman I have ever known. Her consistent companionship and unexplainable love for me remain profound treasures in my life. I love her now more than the day we married and look forward to spending the rest of my life with her. Thank you, Lisa, for all you do and for making this journey with me to the ends of the earth.

My staff has been especially understanding and helpful as I have labored to finish this project. All of them—Victoria, Nathan, Gil, Robin, Connie, Abi (who helped with the research) and Roger—are a dream team, and I thank God for them. Kay and Perry Horner are great friends and have served the Lord with us for many years. Kay helped edit the manuscript and smooth its rough places, making it sound better than I ever could have.

Everyone at Baker's Chosen Books division has been wonderful to work with. Jane Campbell's call of inquiry was the nudge that I needed to complete this book I had been planning for more than a year, and Catherine Cooker's accurate editorial work has been a blessing.

The inspirational discussion moment that launched the Empowered21 initiative happened with two good friends and fellow Oral Roberts University board members, Mart Green and Rob Hoskins. Their insights and courage to ask the tough questions pushed me down the road of discovery that led to more clearly hearing the cry of this generation for spiritual fathers and mothers.

Finally, for all who have helped in any way on *Father Cry*, I want to thank you for your graciousness to me and for standing with me in healing hearts and lives for the Father.

Introduction

The Beatles were one of the great music sensations of the twentieth century. They emerged from the clubs of Liverpool, England, and Hamburg, Germany, to ignite a fan base that was unprecedented in the 1960s. "Beatlemania" grew to a worldwide phenomenon, and in many ways the Beatles became icons of the '60s generation. Anti-establishment expression accompanied by drugs and extreme sexual freedom characterized this time in American and English youth culture, with the Beatles leading the way. George, Paul, Ringo and John became household names.

The social revolution of the '60s also changed established institutions like marriage in ways never before seen in America. Moral deterioration was catapulted from Strawberry Fields and the stages of Woodstock into mainstream American life, and we would never be the same. Advancements in birth control, women working outside of the home, attitudes regarding the unborn and a general spiritual decline during this unique season all dramatically affected American families. The cost of this revolution is still being paid among the children of those most affected by the cultural attitudes that marked the '60s.

This book is not merely about nuclear family deterioration and its effect on today's young people. Although I include some insights on this, you will read much more about a global spiritual phenomenon that I refer to as the cry for spiritual fathers and mothers. The term *spiritual fathers and mothers* does not just refer to biological parents who are very spiritual. Rather, this title will be applied to Christian adults who mentor younger generations in what we call intergenerational mentoring. Spiritual parenting is a biblical principle that is highly valued by God.

Father Cry is intended both for those who are crying out for spiritual fathers and mothers and for those who long to respond to the cry. I will talk a great deal about spiritual fathers. This does not negate the need for spiritual mothers. In fact, *spiritual mothers* could be plugged in after *spiritual fathers* in almost every instance. If you are a woman reading this book, please do not be offended when I fail to put both father and mother in certain passages. In reality we need spiritual mothers as much as spiritual fathers in this generation. It will take all of us working together to make a dent in answering the cry we are hearing around the world.

In addition I will try to blend research and biblical insights with my own very personal story. Parts of this book offer an intimate look into my life, and I will share many things for the very first time. Thank you for allowing me to be vulnerable. My prayer is that my openness will minister to your heart and bring God's healing to your life. If you cry at certain points of the story, then join the crowd. I cried often as I wrote certain sections. Ultimately I pray for two things: First, that through *Father Cry* you will experience God's love in a way that heals your heart. Second, that you will be motivated to heal the hearts of this generation by the power of our Father's love.

During the 1960s, America not only experienced a social and musical revolution but also a spiritual revolution. Throughout this tumultuous decade the movement known as Pentecostalism spread in unusual ways and in unusual places. Mainline denominations began to experience spiritual renewal accompanied by supernatural manifestations. The *charismata*, or "grace gifts" of God, were being witnessed in new places, including among Catholics. A new term, *charismatic*, was coined to identify this wave of grace on the Church. The charismatic movement spread like wildfire in many places, with the Holy Spirit touching millions around the world.

You will notice that while the word *Pentecostal* is capitalized throughout *Father Cry*, the word *charismatic* will always appear in lowercase. This should not be taken in any way as a sign of lesser emphasis on the charismatic movement or charismatic ministries around the world. There are actually more people who would call themselves "charismatic" than those who call themselves "Pentecostal." The lowercase is simply a sign of my submission to Chosen Books. Their style manual and rules would not allow me to capitalize *charismatic* despite my best attempts. Thank you to all my charismatic friends for your understanding.

Most importantly, you will notice in the book the adoption of new language that brings both Pentecostal and charismatic together in unity under the banner *Spirit-empowered*. Hopefully this and other new language that is emerging in contemporary Christianity will help us bridge any gaps between us so we can unite to touch our generation with the power of the Holy Spirit.

One person who helped bridge the gap between the Pentecostal and charismatic movements many years ago was a healing evangelist named Oral Roberts. Oral became one of the most well-known leaders of the Spirit-empowered movement in the twentieth century. A long list of outstanding Pentecostal and charismatic leaders were associated with Oral over the years. He started his ministry in a historic Pentecostal denomination and transitioned to leadership in the charismatic renewal. Yet Oral's work influenced and affected people across all denominations. His ministry of healing was world renowned.

Less renowned at the time, but no less prolific, was Oral's ability to mentor and influence young people for Christ. Young world changers were produced at the university bearing his name, and their influence in taking healing to "every person's world" continues globally to this day. While the Beatles were rising to prominence in the secular world, Oral was being raised up by God in the spiritual world. These two worlds were bound to collide, and they did.

On March 4, 1966, during the height of Beatlemania, John Lennon was interviewed for an article in the *London Evening Standard* about the Beatles' popularity and the world craze swirling around them. John had immersed himself in the study of religion before the interview and wanted to say something about Christianity:

> Christianity will go. It will vanish and shrink. I needn't argue with that; I'm right and I will be proved right. We're more popular than Jesus now; I don't know which will go first—rock 'n' roll or Christianity. Jesus was all right but his disciples were thick and ordinary. It's them twisting it that ruins it for me.[1]

When the American press picked up on this statement, a furor erupted. Many radio stations even banned Beatles music from their playlists.

Lennon's prophecy that "Christianity will go" has, of course, been proven wrong, and within just four years of his controversial interview the Beatles broke up, with the band members starting individual careers. During an Oral Roberts University chapel service on January 26, 1973, Chancellor Roberts read a unique letter and announced a donation he had received from John Lennon to the university. Roberts prefaced the letter by sharing that Lennon's cousin Marilyn McCabe was a partner with Roberts's ministry. Oral also related that he had been praying for Lennon. After writing a letter to Lennon, he received the letter he would share (excerpted):

Dear Rev. Roberts,
This is ex-Beatle, John Lennon. I have been wanting to write to you but I guess I didn't really want to face reality. I never do. . . . Reality frightens me and paranoids me. . . . Let me begin to say, I regret that I said the Beatles were more popular than Jesus. . . .
Here's my life. Born in Liverpool, my mom died when I was little, my father left me at three. It was rough because just my aunt raised me. . . . I had an unhappy childhood, depressed a lot. Always missing my mom. Maybe if I'd had a father like you, I would have been a better person. . . . Married Cynthia, had a son John. . . . Only one regret, John has had to suffer a lot. . . . He and me never get to see each other. . . . So, life as a Beatle hasn't been all that great. . . . As the song we wrote, Paul and me, said, "Money Can't Buy Me Love," it's true. The point is this, I want happiness. I don't want to keep up with drugs. . . . Explain to me what Christianity can do for me? Is it phony? Can he love me? I want out of hell.

Sincerely,
John[2]

18

A *father cry* was ringing out from Lennon's letter to Oral Roberts, a cry for someone who cared and would help him. Lennon wrote, "Maybe if I'd had a father like you, I would have been a better person." After reading the letter, Oral related to the chapel students some of his response to Lennon in future correspondence. Roberts shared the Gospel with Lennon and encouraged him to receive Jesus as his Savior. Within four years, Lennon apparently did just that and was converted to Christ for a short time.[3] Lennon's life, however, was soon overtaken by darkness once again. In 1980 Lennon was shot in the back three times by Mark Chapman outside of his New York City apartment building. Still alive, he climbed the apartment steps and called out. Rushed to the hospital in a police car, Lennon was pronounced dead shortly thereafter. We do not know what happened in Lennon's heart during those last fleeting moments of life. Only God knows Lennon's eternity for sure, but we do know he had a chance because a spiritual father to many young men and women cared enough to reach out.

Fast-forward to the twenty-first century, and we find a generation whose cry for spiritual fathers is ringing loudly around the world. They need someone who will care, someone who will reach out to them, someone to be spiritual fathers or mothers in their lives. This book is about this cry as well as the cry for Father in your own heart. My prayer is that as you read the pages of *Father Cry*, God's love will heal your heart and His Spirit will empower you to bring healing to the hearts of those you love.

1

Father Cry

About three in the afternoon Jesus cried out in a loud voice, "Eli, Eli, lema sabachthani?" (which means "My God, my God, why have you forsaken me?").

Matthew 27:46

Holidays at my grandparents' home were amazing. Every year we would begin the merriment just before Thanksgiving by decorating the entire yard and house. We built a life-size stable with a manger, outlined the roof in lights, carefully placed figurines near the chimney, hung lit stars on poles, adorned the trees and even found a way to decorate the sidewalks. Every year we found some new way to celebrate the birth of Jesus and, of course, the coming of Santa Claus. People came from miles around during the holidays just to see our yard. On the Friday following Thanksgiving, we began work inside the house. Several Christmas trees were decorated, garland hung, manger scenes placed, snowmen unwrapped and Santas from around the world positioned in various locations. Shopping excursions were enjoyed, gift wrapping was celebrated, food was more than abundant and Christmas was king.

My maternal grandmother's name was Mammy. Actually her name was Margaret Collins, but everyone in her world knew her as Mammy. At the age of five, I came to live with her and my grandfather, Henry—or "Pop" as we called him—in their Kentucky home because my parents were getting a divorce. Until I was nineteen, I lived with Mammy and Pop along with my two sisters and mom. I would move from the warmth and love of Mammy's house to college and then immediately into full-time ministry.

Mammy was infatuated with Christmas; what great memories this infatuation would generate for our entire family. Mammy's love for the holidays may have started with her desire to make life special for her three grandchildren. Or it may have grown from the impoverished soil of her Great Depression days, when Christmas celebrations were austere. Perhaps Christmas was the highlight of the year in our home because Mammy and Pop became Christians through an associate pastor's visit and prayer for them on Christmas Eve.

Whatever the reason, it was great to be a recipient of Christmas cheer in the Collins home. Some of my best childhood memories involve that special time of the year. Yet two very difficult moments also happened around the holidays—moments that gave form to a cry in my heart and that ultimately led me to write this book. A long time passed before I realized that what was happening inside of me was an inner longing, an internal scream for parental covering. Through the years, from the core of my being, I would find my heart crying out for a father. The contrast between the warmth of Mammy's house and this cry was stark.

I was born into a preacher's home. My dad was a pastor and minister in a Pentecostal denomination. Ultimately, after his father suffered a stroke, Dad took his father's place as the state supervisor for the denomination in West Virginia. He was very young for this responsibility, and his youthful inexperience would soon be revealed. After serving three years in West Virginia, he walked out of the state parsonage, leaving Mom and three children behind. Within two weeks we were required to move because a new leader was sent to take my father's place. I was five when we packed an old open-bed truck with our stuff for the move to Mammy and Pop's. From that moment forward, I would grow up in a "broken" home, although in the 1960s it was difficult to know all that would mean.

Mom and Dad eventually divorced, becoming greatly estranged. Someone has said, "Divorce is worse than death," and that is true. In divorce you feel the pain of abandonment but without a funeral for closure. Both of my parents suffered the elongated procession of emotions divorce brings, as did my sisters and I.

Mammy and Pop's home was a great place for a child to grow up, but I still bore many of the scars that come from living with one parent absent. Broken trust, inner uncertainty, trauma, guilt, anger and emotional difficulty all became part of my life. Going from my earliest days of Christian bliss and safety in West Virginia to a childhood of vulnerability would take its toll, and it required years of exposure to God's grace to untangle the web of emotions that was woven in those early years of brokenness.

Throughout these years, I learned the meaning of *father cry*.

When I was approximately nine years old, Dad came to visit us for Christmas after a long absence from our lives. Gifts were given and pleasantries exchanged, and then Dad was to leave again. I guess, in some way, I had more than I could handle, and I began to cry for him to stay. My crying actually turned into a wail of anguish. Although I do not remember all the details of the moment, I do remember those hours of crying for my father not to leave me again. Surrounded by holiday tinsel and light, my heart could only feel darkness. The pent-up energy of four years of pain came out in one huge gush of emotion. I cried until my chest heaved off the bed as I begged for someone to keep my father from walking out the door. This was a *father cry*. It was deep. It was passionate. It was messy, and it was desperate.

My earthly father left Mammy's house that night, to my young dismay. My grief continued. It was a long, long night for a little boy. I did not understand at such a young age that Dad could not stay, considering the circumstances and the divorce. His reaction seemed cold and calculated. I would learn much more about what was happening behind the scenes, beyond my childhood eyes, later in life.

The story of our family continued to take numerous twists and turns with several surprising results. God did not leave me on that bed all alone. However, on that night of anguish, my father's reaction only increased my pain. My mother, grandmother and two sisters were frozen by their own heartache. While hurting deeply, they could only observe as my body quaked with emotion. No one really knew what to do to heal my heart. I think we were all just too wounded and torn to help one another. The next day, life continued, the sun rose, laughter returned. My longing cry for father went beneath the surface, but it would not go away for many years.

Another encounter with this *father cry* came at the end of another Christmas celebration. By this time I was an adult, living away from home with my own family. We still enjoyed visiting Mammy's house and gorging ourselves on Christmas cheer. This particular year was less joyous, however, because my grandfather had been struggling with pain. Pop did not celebrate Christmas with the family, and on the day after Christmas, we decided to take him to the hospital.

Henry Collins was an unusual man. He was raised in the Ozark Mountains and knew how to work hard. He was the principal breadwinner of the home, who willingly undertook the support of his three grandchildren when they moved in along with his only daughter, my mom. Pop took us to church, provided the money needed to run the home and served as implementation engineer for my grandmother's continuous home-improvement designs. Pop was called to preach, but he did most of his preaching to us kids and to others who would listen along the way while he made a good living for his enlarged family. Pop was also called to serve. He chauffeured me to ball games, kept me in church, helped me learn to ride horses and taught me much about life. He was a good man, and yet he struggled spiritually, especially in his later years. Darkness never gives up on us. Although I did not know it, Pop had been struggling significantly just before his Christmas illness.

In the few days following that difficult Christmas celebration, the reality of Pop's condition became clearer. His stomach had been punctured in a recent endoscopic procedure, allowing the gastric acids to leak onto his organs. Because of this internal trauma, his body went into septic shock, which meant his system was shutting down. For more than sixty days, Pop remained in the hospital but was unable to receive nutrients by any means. Although he was lucid, he basically starved to death before his family's eyes. Pop was such a strong man that his heart simply refused to stop beating for a long time. Finally, Pop quietly went home to be with the Lord after God had used his two months of illness to prepare him and others for his departure.

My grandfather was the first really close relative of mine to die. God's comforting presence was tangible in the immediate aftermath of his death. Grace was there for me to support my grandmother, mother and other family members. I preached at Pop's funeral and was proud to share the story of the sacrificial love that Pop embodied. Following the funeral and family dinner, my wife, Lisa, and I were at Mammy and Pop's house, the same house in which I was raised. Memories seemed to come at me from every tree, every flower, the lake where we fished, the yard we decorated for Christmas, the barn, the smells, the sounds. . . . All of them reminded me of Pop.

Then, unexpectedly, there it was again—the *father cry*. From somewhere beyond me, it came gushing through my adult frame. Poor Lisa must have been frightened as I bent over double in the yard, mourning Pop's passing. The man who had stepped into my father void was now gone, and an unexpected primal grief was being released. It was desperate. It was messy.

Many years have passed since Pop's home going and since that long Christmas night of crying for my father to stay. Yet I will never forget the emotions I experienced in those moments of longing for a father. These deep, primal emotions inform my heart regarding the *father cry* presently occurring in today's generation of youth. The longing for spiritual covering among young people around the world is deep. It can be messy, and it is definitely desperate. We are witnessing this cry inside and outside of the Church. We also hear this cry in both our physical and spiritual families. Where are the godly fathers? Where are the mothers who will provide covering and nurture to their own? Why does this generation feel so abandoned? Where are the spiritual leaders who will walk with them, for whom they are crying?

A few years after Pop's death, this *father cry* resurfaced in a way I did not expect. This time I was not at my grandparents' home, and it was not the Christmas season; it was cold outside, and I was walking more than a mile just to reach my own home. No, I did not have to walk uphill both ways through several feet of snow to get to school when I was growing up. This was a once-in-a-lifetime moment—thank God! The falling snow had made the roads slick, and my small truck would not make it over the large hill that led to the driveway of my house. With no other choice, I parked the truck and started the long, over-the-hill walk to the warmth of Lisa's kitchen. The snow, the cold, the dreary sky—all seemed to fit well with the condition of my heart in that moment. Tears streamed down my cheeks, partially freezing as they fell.

Why the tears? Beyond the freezing cold that was cutting through my clothes with ferocity, my heart was unexpectedly broken. I was returning from a church meeting in which one of my spiritual fathers, the man I trusted most in the world, had just betrayed me in front of a significant group of my peers. Although his decisions and statements seemed logical and thorough, they did not make "father" sense, nor were they spoken out of love. I was hurting. Parental wounds go deep, including those from spiritual parents.

Emotions flooded my heart, and dozens of thoughts were running through my mind as I trudged along in the ever-deepening snow. *Why did he do that? Did he really mean to hurt me? What did I do wrong? Did I trust him too much? Should I have responded to him in a better way? Can I ever trust him again?*

Following years on my own ministry leadership journey, I have a better understanding of how this kind of moment can happen as a reaction to "leadership" pressure. I am also confident I have wounded spiritual sons and daughters myself through my reactions or decisions I made without carefully weighing my response from a "fatherly" perspective. We would all do well to remember that positions and leadership assignments come and go, but our deeper spiritual relationships with others are meant to last a lifetime.

All of us get wounded, usually by those closest to us. Yet, in the moment of that wounding from a perceived spiritual father, I felt alone in my pain, much like that night of crying for my earthly father not to leave, or my gush of primal grief at Pop's passing. I was not, however, alone in my *father cry*. We never are—heaven understands.

Jesus Himself knows what it is like to cry out for a father. He wept aloud several times during His ministry, such as outside the tomb of His friend Lazarus (John 11:35, 41–42) or in the Garden of Gethsemane (Luke 22:39–46). Yet Christ's most poignant *father cry* came from the cross.

The sky was dark. The pain was excruciating. The crowd was gawking. The soldiers were gambling; and Jesus was dying. Though surrounded by dozens of people, the aloneness of the cross was crushing. Every sin in human history converged on His body, compressing His heart. In that moment of moments, Christ's humanity seemed to be overwhelmed by it all until He finally screamed out, *"Eli, Eli, lema sabachthani?"* (Mark 15:34).

This cry is recorded by both Matthew and Mark in the Aramaic language, the language of the common people; most believe it was the language spoken by Jesus. Several other words and phrases in the New Testament retain the Aramaic pronunciation, including the word *Abba*, used by Jesus in the Garden of Gethsemane. These Aramaic phrases connect us with the intimacy revealed in Jesus' cry in the garden and in His cry from the cross. Christ's impassioned question from the cross was, "My God, My God, why have You forsaken me?" God's only begotten Son was crying for the fellowship of His Father during His greatest moment of need.

This *father cry* from our Savior still reverberates through history, assuring each of us common men and women of His compassion. Jesus understands the cry occurring in this generation: "During the days of Jesus' life on earth, he offered up prayers and petitions with fervent cries and tears to the one who could save him from death, and he was heard because of his reverent submission" (Hebrews 5:7).

Perhaps you know this *father cry* because you have felt forsaken by one who was a spiritual father or mother to you. Some spiritual fathers and mothers simply do not know how to be good spiritual parents. They do not want to intentionally hurt you; rather it is their own inadequacies conveyed through their actions—or lack of action—that impact your heart. Beginning the night that I trudged through the snow, I discovered the person I thought was my spiritual father did not see himself in that role, nor was he good at it. We would have a good relationship beyond that moment, but it would never be quite the same.

The residual pain in today's world, caused by both natural and spiritual wounding, should not be underestimated. Whether through the abandonment, abuse, neglect or alienation of our natural parents or through the moral failure, self-centeredness, insensitivity and rejection of our spiritual parents, this pain is real, and it is pervasive. We must recognize, however, a deep, transformational cry that transcends parentally induced pain; it is a rising call from new generations for spiritual mothers and fathers in the twenty-first century. This cry has the potential to bring a reformation in today's institutions and a spiritual revolution in the earth. At times the cry lurks silently beneath a myriad of human activity, and at other times it swirls tumultuously near the surface of our existence. This cry is pervasive, persistent, passionate and sometimes messy. It must be answered—our legacy depends on it. It is a *father cry*.

2

Awakening to the Cry

He will turn the hearts of the fathers to their children, and the hearts of the children to their fathers; or else I will come and strike the land with total destruction.

Malachi 4:6, NIV1984

Peter and his companions were very sleepy, but when they became fully awake, they saw his glory.

Luke 9:32

Christmastime typically provides a season of respite for me. Traveling for the year is complete, relatives are near and my relaxation mode kicks in. Most years, food, family, fun and football fill these wonderful days of rest. My spirituality is generally not at a high peak as at other times of the year, when I am focusing more on intercession, fasting and advancing the ministry.

I know this should not necessarily be true, but it is. Of course, sometimes God speaks to us even when we are not listening as well as we should. This happened to me a few years ago.

I was emerging from the holiday season and was headed toward a New Year's ministry gathering, where I was scheduled to preach on the future of the Pentecostal movement among new generations in the twenty-first century. Keeping with my custom, I had enjoyed turkey, toys, toddlers and television more than normal while entertaining our family. Now I was on an airplane headed toward my first preaching assignment of the new year and was trying to push my way into a new season of ministry.

I had gratefully accepted an upgrade on the flight and was scheduled to sit in first class. As I placed my carry-on luggage overhead, I grabbed my Bible and planned to continue studying for the imminent preaching assignment. Then I noticed a young man sitting by the window next to my aisle seat. He was Hispanic and looked to be in his late teens—baggy jeans, contemporary T-shirt, piercings and all. As soon as I was seated, the young man asked, "Is that a Bible?"

I replied that it was, to which he responded, "I need that!"

This should have been an immediate sign to me. In the past I have witnessed to several people who have received Christ on airplanes. Normally I would have recognized this as a divine appointment and moved quickly into my evangelistic gifting and call. Nevertheless, you will remember I was full of turkey, toys and television! After a few pleasant words with the young man, I put up my invisible airplane communication shield and quickly fell asleep, Bible in hand.

Suddenly I was awakened as the plane began its descent; I felt as if someone had hit me or nudged me in the side, prodding me awake. The Holy Spirit then spoke to me, reminding me of the young man sitting beside me and the opportunity I was missing. I awakened and began doing what I should have done initially, which was to engage this weary-looking young man in conversation and minister to him.

His name was Gabriel. He had been reared in a pastor's home, but now, barely old enough to be out on his own, he was moving to the East Coast because he had encountered trouble with his peers in a Midwestern state. Gabriel knew he needed God's Word, but he did not know much about it. In fact, though he lived in a ministry setting, Gabriel was not aware of how to personally become a Christian believer. I shared a simple Gospel message, and he allowed me to pray for him, though he did not receive Christ that day. I continued talking to Gabriel until our luggage arrived at the baggage claim. I left the airport, grieving in my heart that I had wasted my initial opportunity to share what Gabriel knew he needed.

The next morning I was in prayer in my hotel room, reflecting and studying for the sermon I would preach at the conference. I was still grieving over my inability to help Gabriel receive Christ when I believe the Holy Spirit spoke to me: *Yesterday, I gave you a living illustration of what is happening with new generations in America.* This captured my attention, and so I listened intently to the impression I was receiving from the Lord. *There is a new generation hungry for My Word and desperately needing spiritual help. Yet older generations are sleeping through their moment of opportunity without responding properly—just like you did on the plane yesterday. They are slumbering because they are too full of the things of this life to hear the cry of this generation, and they need an awakening. The greatest harvest of your time depends on the Church waking from her slumber and reaching them.*

While sharing about this occasion a couple of years later, I suddenly realized the young man had the same name as Gabriel, the messenger angel of Scripture. I would not presume to say that this young man was an angel, but God certainly used him to give me His message that day. The message I received is critical for the Church. Will we wake up and hear the cry of this generation of young men and women? It is a cry for God, a cry for His Word and a cry for fathers and mothers.

This cry is all around us!

In just my life span, we have witnessed the deterioration of the family structure becoming a social reality. Divorce, abuse, abandonment and fatherlessness continue to escalate around the world and especially in the West.[1] Almost two generations of American young people have grown up fatherless. Of children in the United States born since 1984, more than 60 percent will spend an average of five years of their childhood in a single-parent family.[2] In some communities, children only have a one-in-five chance of reaching age sixteen with the same two parents in the home. An alarming 63 percent of black children, 35 percent of Hispanic children and 28 percent of white children are living in homes absent of their fathers[3]; overall more than 24 million children are now living without their biological father present in the home.[4]

Time magazine stated several years ago,

> More children will go to sleep tonight in a fatherless home than ever in the nation's history. Talk to the experts in crime, drug abuse, depression, or school failure, and they can point

to some study somewhere blaming those problems on the disappearance of fathers from the American family.[5]

David Blankenhorn, the founder of the Institute for American Values in New York City, says, "This trend of fatherlessness is the most socially consequential family trend of our generation."[6] He speaks for most Americans: More than 70 percent agree with the notion that absence of fathers from the home is the most significant family or social problem facing the United States.[7] Mothers are not exempt from the story, either, as more mothers are abandoning their children than ever in American history, and two-thirds of all divorces are initiated by women.

The results of this fatherless or parentless situation have been catastrophic. An increase in almost every negative indicator in the lives of children and teenagers is seen when parents are absent from their lives.[8] From drug abuse, to premarital sex, to incarceration, to living below poverty levels, the detrimental effects of parental absenteeism and neglect remain startling.

Many times it is not just the physical abandonment of the father of his home but the emotional abandonment of the father *in* his home that is harmful. We must realize that children need time with their parents and not merely things from them. Sometimes we simply are too busy. One little boy asked his father, "Daddy, how much money do you make?"

The dad was exhausted from a long day at work and really did not want to get into this conversation with his son, so he quickly retorted, "Enough!"

The boy was not satisfied, so he pressed on. "I mean, how much do you make an hour?"

The man was not in the mood for this interrogation, so he gave a quick lecture about not asking these kinds of questions and then grumbled, "They pay me twenty-five dollars an hour."

The young boy, unruffled by his dad's resistance, asked boldly, "Can I borrow ten dollars?"

The father said, "No, now go to sleep!"

The next morning, however, the dad softened, apologized to his son and handed him a ten-dollar bill. The boy's countenance shifted from doom to delight as he held the ten dollars in his hand. Quickly he ran to his room and returned with his own small piggy bank. The father watched as his son poured out the entire contents of the bank on the kitchen table and began to diligently count his change. Finally, the lad pushed all of his pennies, nickels, dimes and quarters toward his father, followed by the prized ten-dollar bill. "Here's 25 dollars, Daddy. Can I buy an hour of your time?"

In a *USA Today* article, actor David Cassidy was interviewed about his life as a teen idol of the 1970s. He played Keith Partridge on the popular television series *The Partridge Family* and was one of the best-known television actors in America during the show's run. David's father was also an actor, but their relationship was not good. His father died in 1976 without knowing the kind of success that David experienced. Cassidy would say about his father, "I was hurt by the fact that he was bitter and jealous of my success. All I wanted him to do was put his arm around me and tell me he loved me."[9]

Children want time and love. The lack of both has affected this generation dramatically. Broken homes have generated broken hearts.

This parental void is a reality of the twenty-first century and provides a sociological context for the father cry we are hearing. In 1989 there were more than four million stepfamilies with minor children in the United States, and it was estimated even then that somewhere between 33 percent and 40 percent of all U.S. children would live in a stepfamily before they reached the age of eighteen.[10] Local churches also have been negatively affected by these trends, with divorces happening at an escalated rate within the church[11] and the influx of stepfamilies and blended families increasing. Thus a significant number of young men and women with exposure to church are living without a stable homelife or strong parental support.

At the same time, many churches are also experiencing a discipleship crisis.[12] In numerous larger churches, younger generations are placed in children's church, youth groups and other isolated entities where adult interaction is limited. This isolation tends to allow for suspicion, misunderstanding and absence of appreciation for other age groups. In a context where many young people have a literal parent void and are attending churches where they have a limited connection with older generations, an understandable sense of need for meaningful relationships with more experienced believers is growing. The environment of nuclear-family deterioration and a rapid transformation in today's Christianity form fertile ground for a radical heart cry for spiritual fathers and mothers.

Broken Trust

Added to these factors are consistent and deep wounds caused by the fall of leaders over the last few decades. In the late 1980s, I was sitting in a hotel lobby in Bangkok, Thailand, reading the local newspaper's report on the Jim Bakker collapse and feeling amazement at how fast bad news travels. This is but one instance in an onslaught of negative revelations about those in authority that has inundated this generation of young people.

They have witnessed atrocities ranging all the way from a U.S. president enduring an impeachment proceeding for sexual sins in the White House to teachers from the local school being indicted for their flings with minors. They are bombarded with messages of failure in leadership. Consequently, the much-publicized collapses of Christian leaders have especially fueled a fire of cynicism that is now rampant. From ministers trading their marriage partners without a moment away from the pulpit, to preachers poaching parishioners' pockets through pompous preaching, to clergy compromising themselves with children—the stories of Christian leadership failures have been paraded in the media. In actuality, ministers and Christian leaders have fallen morally all through the ages; a quick read through Scripture is clear evidence of this. Yet because of the modern media's capacity for immediate disclosure and the public's thirst for sordid details, we appear to have been in a worst-case scenario for moral failure during the last few decades.

The breaking of trust by leaders with this generation of young people is aggravated by the brokenness of family, and vice versa. They are left feeling vulnerable, uncovered and longing for those they can trust. They are yearning for leaders who have integrity, who are authentic and who will provide them with the spiritual covering they cannot seem to find anywhere else.

We who have experienced a level of spiritual maturity in our relationship with Christ must become the spiritual examples new generations desperately need. It is our responsibility to regard authority as a sacred trust that must not be violated with our children and those who follow us. We must become spiritual parents whom this generation can trust. We must also teach today's young men and women how to negotiate the brokenness they are experiencing and find wholeness through the grace of God. One principal grace they will need for this is the ability to forgive.

A few years ago, a student gave a speech at Oral Roberts University about what it meant to attend a university whose vision and mission were about healing and wholeness. Anna* talked about whole people ministering to the whole person. Anna attended Oral Roberts University at a time of transition, brokenness and mistrust; still, she discovered the special grace she needed in her journey toward wholeness. It was an inspiring and touching discourse that stirred her listeners, who included students, faculty and trustees. Almost no one in the audience, however, knew the story of her family, her broken heart and her pathway to healing that lay behind her speech. Anna was kind enough to share some of this with me:

> *In my mind, my childhood resembled the "American dream." I had one mom, one dad, one brother and a dog named Harry, all living together in a very nice suburban home. I have fond memories of family trips to amusement parks, malls and the beach. I do not remember any sort of lack. If I really wanted something—a Barbie doll or new clothes—I simply had to ask. While I experienced typical sibling rivalry, I loved my parents and especially my dad. I was a daddy's girl. Life was great.*
>
> *At a young age I began to notice that many families in our neighborhood were beginning to split up*

*The name of this student has been changed to protect her privacy.

because of divorce. I would see how hard it was on my friends who now spent the weekdays with one parent and the weekends with another. I remember thinking to myself, "I'm so thankful that divorce will never happen to my parents." That innocent thought only proved how oblivious I was to the storm of events that was about to unfold.

At the age of nine my happy little white-picket-fence life came to a screeching halt. My mother had discovered that my dad was having an affair with a close family friend. Little did I know that this was not the first time that my mom had known about my father's infidelity. Within a week my parents were separated, and I went from the American dream to an American statistic. Shortly after the divorce my dad remarried and moved to the other side of town. Unfortunately the divorce bankrupted my mother. Almost overnight we went from a five-bedroom home to a one-bedroom apartment that my mom, my brother and I shared.

I was heartbroken. I could not understand why my dad had done this to me—because in my young mind this could only be something intentional. Did he not see how this would wreck my life? But I was Daddy's girl, and I never intended to confront him with my offense. I did not want to lose my spot as Daddy's girl, especially because he now had stepdaughters that were my competition. Therefore I acted like nothing ever happened. I would just continue to be a sweet little girl that would win his love back. Unfortunately my plan did not work. Over the next few years, as our relationship waned, I noticed that his name was no longer "Daddy" to me. I now referred to him as "my father"—a person who lived in my town, but whom I only saw on occasion.

As my father gained a new family, my brother and I started to lose our place. We saw less and less of him. His new family dictated when we could and could not see our father. My brother and I were overwhelmed with the sense of rejection. Our father chose them over us. In the summer I turned sixteen, my father told my brother and me that he no longer wanted to be our dad and that he never wanted to speak to us again. I was wounded so deeply. I remember saying to my mom, "I will never forgive him."

My wise mother replied, "Anna, someday you're going to have to forgive him, or you will never be able to move on in your life." Although in the moment I would never have admitted it, she turned out to be absolutely right.

It was around that time that I made a conscious decision to make Jesus Lord over my life. As a young child I had prayed the salvation prayer. Jesus had been my Savior for many years, but when I was a teenager, I wanted to be a disciple. In high school I fell in love with Jesus and wanted to serve God for the rest of my life. After graduation I worked for a ministry in Georgia for two years and then went on to Oral Roberts University. I loved God and I loved serving His people. I knew that God had great plans for me. There was a part of my heart, however, that was so hurt and offended. For some reason I was not able to have healthy relationships with men. I saw every man as someone who would inevitably reject me, just like my father did. It was a deep wound that I was happily sweeping under the rug. Those types of wounds do not heal with time, however; time only made my heart grow harder, and the offense just got deeper toward my father. I was desperate to see some change in my life.

I began to ask God about this issue in my heart. I knew that I needed to forgive my father, but I did not really know where to start. After seeking counsel, I got the idea to send my father a letter. I also knew that I needed to pray for him. I remember my first prayers for my father being hard to even speak out. The words "God, please bless my father" felt more like poison coming from my mouth than a sweet petition to the Lord. I know God was well aware of my bitter prayers, but I continued to pray for my father anyway.

Within a few weeks I mustered up the guts to send my father a simple and short letter letting him know that I would like to talk with him. I never received a response. So I decided to write him another letter. In the second letter I told him that I did not want anything from him, that I was just asking for a cordial relationship. I never received a response. After some time I figured my father was perhaps too proud or too timid to respond, but surely he was at least curious about my life. I then wrote him a very long letter telling him all the details of my life that I thought he would at least be interested in knowing. I never received a response.

I continued to pray for my father, and I started to notice my prayers changing. It went from a "God, bring my father to repentance!" to a genuine, heartfelt "Lord, I'm asking that You bless my father's home, his family, his job and everything he touches. God, I ask that You would pour Your love out upon him and draw his heart close to You." I could actually feel my heart attitude change toward him.

Although I had not heard back from my father, I started sending him holiday cards and postcards from some of my travels. I still never received a response. I continued to write him letters for three years. Then finally one day I got something in the mail. It was an envelope that was clearly from my father. In the envelope was every letter, holiday card and postcard that I had sent him, along with a letter from him. In the letter he said that I was "barking up the wrong tree" and that he never wanted to hear from me again.

To someone in my situation, it could have been devastating—the ultimate and final rejection. I had the strangest reaction, however. I was okay. I did cry, but not for long. What I did not realize was that every letter I sent him was a physical manifestation of my heart releasing him from any offense that I had to-ward him. For those three years I was in the process of forgiveness. In this process I had drawn close to my heavenly Father, the One to whom my Spirit now cries out, "Abba, Father." It was then that I realized I was free. My father had no more debt with me. I no longer felt the bitter flame of unforgiveness in my heart every time I thought of him. I actually felt the soft warmth of God's love toward him.

Despite how my father may have felt toward me, I now had peace in my heart toward him. Although I stopped sending him letters, I continued to pray for him. A few years had passed since receiving all my letters back from my father when one day I received an email from him. He simply said, "Anna, I love you. Please forgive me. Love, Dad." Overwhelmed with joy

*that my father had reached out to me, I responded
with love. I told him about how I had forgiven him
a long time ago and that God had healed my heart.*

*Although to this day we do not have any sort of
relationship that goes beyond a few cordial emails, I
continue to pray for him. I know that the same God
who healed my heart is ready to heal my father's heart.
In the meantime, God has become my Father in a
very real way. I go to Him for everything. He is my
provider, my protector, and I'm His little girl.*

Gabriel and Anna's message is clear. Their generation is
hurting, confused and in need. They are looking for people
to help them negotiate life—people who can help them
find healing for their hearts. Who will hear their cry and
become a representative of God with skin on? Who will
teach the principles of love and forgiveness? Who will lead
them to find the answer to their father cry in a relationship
with our heavenly Father? Who? Only those who are awake!

3

Passing the Baton
(Biblically Speaking)

Your sons will take the place of your fathers; you will make them princes throughout the land. I will perpetuate your memory through all generations; therefore the nations will praise you for ever and ever.

Psalm 45:16–17

And the things that thou hast heard of me among many witnesses, the same commit thou to faithful men, who shall be able to teach others also.

2 Timothy 2:2, KJV

The risk-filled moments when one runner passes the baton to another in a relay race are why these races are so exciting. The baton pass is one of the most critical moments of a relay race. If a team expects to win, each runner must successfully place the baton firmly in the hand of the next runner, without breaking stride. Many times races are won or lost in the baton pass—as happened on the next-to-last day of the 2004 Olympic Games in Athens, Greece.

The favored team in the women's 4×100 meter relay, the American team, was headlined by Marion Jones, who had won five Olympic medals at the 2000 Sydney games. By 2004 she was considered the fastest woman in the world and one of the greatest Olympic athletes of all time. In Athens, Jones ran the second leg for her team in the final of the 4×100 meter relay. The Americans ran record times in the preliminaries, and as the team began the final race, everyone thought that they would soon hear the national anthem of the United States in the victory ceremony.

In the 4×100, the runners have a 20-meter passing area in which they must transfer the baton to the next runner. For a brief moment, both runners are moving together as the baton is exchanged. You are not allowed to pass the baton to the next runner before entering the passing zone, and if you fail to make the handoff before you exit the passing area, your team is disqualified. Marion Jones took the baton from the leadoff runner and raced down the track. Jones, who was the oldest member of the team, was to pass the baton to a new young star of the American team named Lauryn Williams, who was running the third leg.

The American team looked as though they were well on their way to a gold medal with Jones far ahead of her nearest competitor as she entered the passing zone. However, young Williams took off too soon. The older Jones seemed weary and could not get the baton passed to Williams. Twice she tried, but she could not make the connection with her teammate within the allotted space given.

The American team was disqualified from the race. The team did not get the gold or even finish because they could not make the needed transition in the proper amount of time. The church of the twenty-first century is in a supernaturally expanded passing zone in which one generation is passing the baton of passion and purpose to another. This is especially true in the global Spirit-filled movement. We must make the needed transitions within the allotted amount of time God has given us or we may be disqualified from the race altogether. Christianity has always been just one generation away from extinction, and that remains true in our day.

The worldwide Spirit-empowered or renewalist movement currently numbers more than six hundred million people.[1] For more than a hundred years, this movement has grown exponentially. Major Pentecostal denominations have now developed into some of the largest and fastest-growing evangelical denominations.[2] Yet, around the world, the movement is in a change mode as it attempts to engage new generations for Christ. My personal opinion is that much of the movement remains in an elongated transitional moment while attempting to fully engage the twenty-first century and all it may mean for Spirit-filled ministry.[3] An emerging generation of young men and women are searching for direction, looking for their place and seeking to make a difference for Christ. In a world and Church whose median age continues to escalate, this rise of new generations has placed pressure on older systems in historic denominations. Leaders and pastors throughout God's Kingdom are responding to these pressures with varying degrees of willingness and success.

Generational misunderstandings have often resulted from diverse age groups finding a large chasm lying between them. Vocabulary, style, dress, music and program disagreements have all resulted in a generational disconnect. These disconnections have left leaders searching for those who will carry forward their legacy. At the same time, young people have been left with the sense that they do not have spiritual fathers and mothers whom they can trust.

In 2008 the ministry I lead began serving a process that would ultimately be called Empowered21. This process began as a function of the Board of Trustees at Oral Roberts University and reflected our desire to ensure the mission of the university into the future. We wanted to know how new generations felt about the issues facing Spirit-filled, charismatic Christians and to look at ways we could respond. As the process began, we soon realized that we had providentially stumbled into a larger discussion, which was very relevant for Spirit-filled, Pentecostal and charismatic—or Spirit-empowered—movements around the world. We embarked on a global tour to listen to leaders, scholars and new generations.

During a 12-month period from December 2008 until December 2009, we held 17 unique conversation events on 5 continents with more than 540 leaders, scholars and new-generation participants. In the process we asked similar questions of each group regarding the future of the Spirit-empowered movement among new generations. Our common findings were used to form the program for an Empowered21 Global Congress on Holy Spirit Empowerment in the Twenty-first Century, which took place in Tulsa, Oklahoma, in April 2010.[4] Several top trends and needs were identified for the future of Spirit-empowered Christianity, including leadership integrity, greater emphasis in pastoral teaching on the Holy Spirit and—most importantly for this book—the need and desire among new generations for spiritual fathers and mothers.[5] This cry for spiritual fathers and mothers was global. Representatives from every continent involved in the conversation expressed this need and actually referred to it using parental language without prior sensitizing. Beyond these regional conversations, we also used focus groups of students at Oral Roberts University to test what we were hearing and probe deeper into what this generation was trying to say. The energy among the students around this issue was greater than for any other subject we engaged.[6] Leaders also expressed their resonance with this need among today's youth and hoped we could find a way to significantly address it. These discoveries have ultimately led me to write this book as a journey of discovery on this issue.

What are spiritual fathers or mothers? What do they do? What kind of people should they be?

Biblical Patterns for Spiritual Fathers and Mothers

The Bible provides numerous opportunities to observe spiritual parents in action. A nuclear family model of teaching and disciple-making is also crucial for the formational success of new generations; there are several of these in Scripture as well. These biblical familial models include examples like Abraham, Isaac and Jacob; Jacob and his twelve sons; Aaron and his sons; Eli and his sons; David and Solomon; Elizabeth, Zechariah and John; Mary, Joseph and Jesus; and Lois, Eunice and Timothy. Biblical models for the nuclear, biological family should be taught and encouraged in Christian communities, since the principal place for disciple-making should be in the home. What I primarily want to explore in this volume, however, are nonfamilial models in which spiritual parenting and intergenerational mentoring occur. The most trustworthy place to find examples of spiritual parenting is in Scripture.

Moses and Joshua

The account of Moses' mentoring relationship with Joshua begins after the exodus from Egypt when Moses selected Joshua to lead the battle with Amalek (Exodus 17). Following this first mention, Joshua's name appears periodically in ways that indicate a close relationship with Moses. Joshua was called Moses' minister and accompanied Moses to Mount Sinai (Exodus 24:13–14). He met Moses on his way down from the mountain (Exodus 32:17). He was called Moses' servant (Numbers 11:28). Joshua served as one of the spies chosen by Moses to go into Canaan and brought back a positive report (Numbers 13, 14). God commanded Moses to position Joshua as his successor, which Moses did (Numbers 27:18, 22). Joshua was lifted up in the eyes of the people and succeeded Moses, leading the Israelites in the conquest of Canaan.

Through these accounts, we witness Joshua fulfilling his destiny and Moses ensuring his legacy. Success without a successor is actually failure. Though he did fail at times, Moses avoided failure by having a viable successor in the person of Joshua. He passed the baton to Joshua during his lifetime, ensuring that God's work would continue into a new generation. Dr. Rickie Moore notes that "Moses is an elder who, in the end, becomes a youth minister. He is a father who functions as a mentor to the children of Israel."[7] This is nowhere more evident than in his mentoring of young Joshua to become a great leader. The intergenerational connection between Moses and Joshua was critical to the successful passage of a new generation into the Promised Land. Time spent together, teaching by example, a life of integrity, the influence of blessing and the power of positive words are all seen in this biblical model.

Naomi and Ruth

Naomi hailed from the little town of Bethlehem, where she lived with her husband, Elimelech, in a time of severe famine. The economy was ravaged, so Elimelech and Naomi felt their only hope was to move someplace where they could make a living. They traveled to the hill country of Moab near the Dead Sea with their two sons, Mahlon and Chilion. There, both sons were married to Moabite girls, named Ruth and Orpah. Their immigration journey ended horribly with Elimelech, Mahlon and Chilion all dying in Moab. Naomi buried her family and then turned her heart toward home; she was ready to return to Bethlehem where the famine had ended. Naomi encouraged her daughters-in-law to remain in Moab and find for themselves new husbands. Orpah agreed and left her mother-in-law, but Ruth would not leave. Ruth committed to Naomi because she loved her and adopted Naomi into a type of spiritual daughter-mother relationship (Ruth 1:16–18).

Ruth accompanied Naomi back to Bethlehem, where they lived together in relative poverty until being redeemed by Boaz (Ruth 3–4). Ruth's marriage to Boaz and the child of their union became a blessing to Naomi in her old age (Ruth 4:13–17). In this spiritual mother/daughter model, Ruth made the commitment of loyalty and faithfulness necessary to be a spiritual daughter. Naomi gave wisdom, insight and discernment to Ruth. As a result Naomi was blessed in her old age by the fruitfulness of her spiritual daughter.

Ruth and Boaz's marriage in Bethlehem produced a son named Obed. He was the father of Jesse and Jesse the father of David, who would become king of Israel. Naomi was blessed to nurse and care for David's grandfather, while Ruth, a Gentile, was grafted in to the family of promise. These blessings culminate in Jesus, who was born in Bethlehem and is from the earthly lineage of David.

The story of Ruth reveals the power of loyalty, the impartation of understanding from the aged and the blessing of a spiritual daughter's fruitfulness. Again, the fulfillment of destiny and legacy occurs in this particular account of spiritual parenting. The story of Ruth and Naomi is an intergenerational testimony of hope in spite of the difficulties of life.[8] God still takes the pain of loss and grief and turns it into joy and blessing, especially when generations love and work together.

Elijah and Elisha

The account of Elijah and Elisha is perhaps the most used scriptural example of the spiritual father/son relationship. Elisha is first mentioned in the life of the prophet Elijah on Mount Horeb, where God instructed Elijah to recruit Elisha to take his place (1 Kings 19:16). Elisha committed to follow Elijah (1 Kings 19:21) and became his minister (2 Kings 3:11). Elisha faithfully followed his mentor until Elijah was caught up into the heavens. At this point we see the true heart of Elisha revealed toward Elijah when he called him his father: "And Elisha saw it, and he cried, *My father, my father,* the chariot of Israel, and the horsemen thereof. And he saw him no more: and he took hold of his own clothes, and rent them in two pieces" (2 Kings 2:12, KJV, emphasis added).

Elisha took up Elijah's mantle and entered into prophetic leadership himself (2 Kings 2). This prophetic intergenerational succession forms a model that reveals much regarding spiritual fathers and mothers. We learn that spiritual sons must make a commitment, be willing to submissively serve, continue to be loyal through difficulties, be with the mentor and be willing to assume responsibility as needed. We also learn that spiritual fathers must clearly hear God's voice in selecting those whom they will adopt as spiritual sons, live in a way that inspires emulation, continue faithful to the call of God upon their lives, leave something for the next generation to take up and allow their spiritual sons the access needed to succeed. So much can be gleaned from the relationship of Elijah and Elisha that I will return to them throughout this book.

Mordecai and Esther

The book of Esther is an account that principally takes place in the courts of Persia at the palace of King Xerxes. Esther, a Jewish orphan, was adopted by her cousin Mordecai, a Benjamite and relative of King Saul (Esther 2:5–7). Mordecai became Esther's spiritual father and guide in one of the most intriguing and dangerous times of Israel's history. Mordecai pushed Esther forward toward her destiny of becoming queen (Esther 2:8). He consistently checked in on her to know how she was doing (Esther 2:11). He instructed her with wisdom regarding how she should handle her identity as a Jew (Esther 2:20). He provided information to help her succeed as queen (Esther 2:21–23). Mordecai demonstrated integrity in refusing to bow to Haman, the Agagite (Esther 3:1–2). He challenged Esther at appropriate times and gave himself to prayer and fasting for her (Esther 4). Mordecai stood by Esther in victory and served with her as well as served her (Esther 9).

We see in Esther several things worthy of emulation in spiritual daughters, including a teachable spirit, a willingness to be challenged, a reliance on the prayers of her spiritual father and the courage to step forward into her God-ordained place of service. This intergenerational team of spiritual father and spiritual daughter together changed the world, saving Israel from annihilation.

Paul and Timothy

The apostle Paul was a spiritual father in the early Church. He notes his "fathership" to the Corinthian believers: "For though ye have ten thousand instructors in Christ, yet have ye not many fathers: for in Christ Jesus I have begotten you through the gospel" (1 Corinthians 4:15, KJV). Although he was an apostolic spiritual father for many early Christian communities, Paul's personal spiritual fathering role is seen most clearly in his relationship with Timothy. Paul, heeding the advice of the brethren at Lystra and Iconium, selected Timothy to travel with his ministry team (Acts 16:2). Timothy came from a family in which his mother was a believer and his father was not (Acts 16:1). Timothy had a strong Christian heritage from his mother, Eunice, and his grandmother, Lois (2 Timothy 1:5). Yet Timothy needed a spiritual father in order to reach his full potential in Christ. Paul called Timothy his son (1 Timothy 1:2, 18; 2 Timothy 1:2; 2:1) in the faith.

The model of Paul and Timothy is one of the clearest in Scripture for defining the roles of spiritual parents and spiritual children. The writings recorded in 1 and 2 Timothy are instructions of a spiritual father to his spiritual son, and Timothy's faithful discharge of service is a prime example of the commitment needed by spiritual sons and daughters. Timothy served Paul in the good times and the bad (Acts 16). Timothy could be trusted (Philippians 2:19–20). Timothy was empowered by Paul to do the work of ministry (1 Timothy) and was corrected by Paul in the midst of that work (2 Timothy). At the end of his journey, Paul's spiritual son, Timothy, ministered to the aged apostle (2 Timothy 4:9–21).

Intergenerational Mentoring in the Early Church

The early Christian Church used intergenerational mentoring for discipleship and formational purposes. The book of Titus gives us one glimpse of this in the second chapter, in which the "aged" women are instructed to teach the young women. "Then they can urge the younger women to love their husbands and children, to be self-controlled and pure, to be busy at home, to be kind, and to be subject to their husbands, so that no one will malign the word of God" (Titus 2:4–5).

This pattern of older believers instructing the younger was seen both in Hebrew history and in the Greek/Roman world surrounding early Christian ministry. The Old Testament clearly outlines the pattern of instructing children and elders teaching younger people the ways of the Lord (Deuteronomy 11:18–21; Psalm 145:4; Joel 1:3). The Greek and Roman world also used the apprenticeship method to introduce a younger person into an occupation. The wisdom of aged teachers like Socrates and Plato was sought by younger philosophers, so the pattern of the older teaching the younger was well established in the world surrounding the early Church.[9] Paul and others either adopted this model from the Old Testament or from practical concerns for continuation. By the conclusion of the writing of the New Testament, the pattern of intergenerational mentoring was becoming well established in early Church practice.

Christianity has survived throughout history because one generation has passed the faith on to another. Sometimes we have been more successful at this than at other times. The twenty-first century has brought us to a new season of spiritual transition, one in which the younger generation must not move too fast and the older generation must push themselves to get the baton passed. We are intersecting together in God's passing zone. If we follow the pattern of Scripture, spiritual fathers and mothers will not fail to impart to their spiritual sons and daughters the passion, purpose and purity needed to finish the race. Together we can win. Apart we will be disqualified.

4

Generation to Generation

Then the LORD passed by in front of him and pro-claimed, "The LORD, the LORD God, compassion-ate and gracious, slow to anger, and abounding in lovingkindness and truth; who keeps loving-kindness for thousands, who forgives iniquity, transgression and sin; yet He will by no means leave the guilty unpunished, visiting the iniquity of fathers on the children and on the grandchil-dren to the third and fourth generations."

Exodus 34:6–7, NASB

Because hands were lifted up against the throne of the LORD, the LORD will be at war against the Amalekites from generation to generation.

Exodus 17:16, emphasis added

My paternal grandmother was a preacher. Born into a family full of alcoholics and agnostics, Bessie Amos Wilson was converted at an early age and began to preach soon thereafter. In the early to mid-1900s, Bessie traveled through America as an evangelist with great results. One of these great results was finding a husband. My grandfather, M. E. Wilson, was converted during one of Bessie's meetings, and they were soon married. Bessie was a fireball and a very effective soul winner.

One year Bessie preached in the mountains of Virginia, conducting a two-week revival at a small local church. To say the revival did not go well would be an understatement; in fact, Bessie would say this was the worst revival that she ever conducted. She preached for two entire weeks, and only one child was converted to Christ. Years later, during a large conference, my grandmother met a beautiful young woman, neatly dressed and carrying her Bible. The young lady asked, "Sister Wilson, do you remember preaching in a small church in the mountains of Virginia several years ago?"

Bessie replied, "I sure do, honey. That was the worst revival I have ever conducted in my entire ministry. I preached two whole weeks without any results."

The young lady quickly responded, "Oh, Sister Wilson, please don't say that. I was the one little girl who accepted Jesus as my Savior during that revival, and now I am also a preacher."

This young preacher, whose name was Maude, married a minister and served for years by his side. The Martins were pastors, evangelists and denominational leaders. In the latter years of their life, this elderly tag team continued preaching together, even after they retired, at revivals in local churches—one of them being the church I attended during my first year of marriage.

My wife, Lisa, came from a different denominational background than I did. I tell people that Lisa helped me find Jesus, and I helped her discover the power of the Holy Spirit. We had been married for about a year when the Martins came to visit the church. Maude and her husband took turns every night preaching. Each night of the revival, Lisa would linger in prayer, seeking more of God and asking for the fullness of the Holy Spirit in her life.

Because of the teaching she received in her former denomination, Lisa had difficulty breaking through. She tried numerous approaches during the weeklong revival: long prayers, short prayers, fasting, crying, singing, praying alone and praying with others. None of it left her spiritually satisfied. Later Lisa would recognize that she did not need to do all this work to receive God's free gift. During this revival, however, she needed help.

Maude preached on the last night of the meeting, and after ministering from the pulpit, she spent time ministering to Lisa. In a short while Lisa moved from frustration to elation, experiencing the power of the Holy Spirit in a very personal way. It was a glorious experience for Lisa and has been glorious to her ever since. She has walked consistently in a beautiful dynamic of grace since the night Maude gently and wisely ministered to her. A young girl saved under my grandmother's ministry consequently helped lead my wife into a lifetime of spiritual power. The lesson is simple: What we do for Christ is never wasted, and many times what is done in one generation will not be reaped or corrected until another generation.

An Intergenerational Fight

We see this principle clearly in God's dealings with the Amalekites. First mentioned in the book of Genesis, the Amalekites were a nomadic people living in the Sinai wilderness who, during several generations, came into conflict with the Israelite people. One striking characteristic of the Amalekites is that they did not fight fair. They always attacked when people were weak and in their most vulnerable moments.

In Exodus 17 the Israelites emerged from Egyptian bondage and were headed for the Promised Land. Pharaoh's decimated army was behind them, and Canaan was before them. By the time they reached the valley of Rephidim, the Israelites were weary and vulnerable when the Amalekites attacked. Moses sent his spiritual son Joshua into the battle, while he climbed to the top of the mountain. Joshua led Israel onto the physical battlefield, and Moses led Israel onto the spiritual battlefield. When Moses lifted the rod of his authority to God, Joshua won the battle in the valley, but when Moses let his hands down, Joshua and Israel lost. Positive momentum was dependent on intercession. In this intergenerational battle, both Moses and Joshua were needed for victory.

Moses did his job, and Joshua did his. Together they defeated the Amalekites, turning away their aggression. These two generations were in unity. By the end of the long day of battle in the valley of Rephidim, God had formed a new intergenerational army. He empowered strategic leadership for the conquest of the Promised Land and simultaneously revealed a multigenerational enemy.

Following the victory over Amalek, Moses built an altar and called it "The Lord is My Banner." Then Moses said, "Because hands were lifted up against the throne of the Lord, the Lord will be at war against the Amalekites from *generation to generation*" (Exodus 17:16, emphasis added). From this battle, which required the participation of two generations to win, Moses declared that God would be at war with Amalek for generations to come. The reasons for this amazing proclamation are found later, in the book of Deuteronomy, in one of the sternest biblical declarations ever made against a nation or people group:

> Remember what the Amalekites did to you along the way when you came out of Egypt. When you were weary and worn out, they met you on your journey and attacked all who were lagging behind; they had no fear of God. When the LORD your God gives you rest from all the enemies around you in the land he is giving you to possess as an inheritance, you shall blot out the name of Amalek from under heaven. Do not forget!
>
> Deuteronomy 25:17–19

Blot out the name of Amalek from under heaven! What a pronouncement of judgment! Future generations were to finish what started in the wilderness of Sinai. Because Amalek attacked when Israel was weary and worn, because they attacked their weak spot first, because they did not fear God and because they tried to keep the people of God from their destiny, they were to be destroyed by future generations. What one generation starts, another generation must often complete.

Leaving Work Unfinished

In the history of the United States, two families have had a father and son both serve as president of the United States. John Adams served as our second president, and his son John Quincy Adams served as our sixth. The only other family whose father and son both held the United States' highest office was the Bush family, one of the great political families in American history.

The presidencies of George H. W. Bush and George W. Bush graphically illustrated, for the world to see, how generations may be tied to one another. On January 17, 1991, a massive air and missile attack on Iraq, named Operation Desert Storm, was begun by the United States. Iraqi leader Saddam Hussein had used his army to invade Kuwait in August 1990 because of disputes over oil and land. Iraq defeated Kuwait's army and occupied the nation. The United Nations established sanctions against Iraq, warning Hussein and Iraq to pull out of Kuwait by January 15, 1991. The deadline passed without Iraqi withdrawal, and war began! Desert Storm was a huge success for the American and allied forces. In slightly more than a month, the Iraqi army was routed, and the Iraqis were withdrawing from their occupation of Kuwait.

Though Kuwait's freedom was restored, Saddam Hussein remained in power. Many in the United States questioned openly why President George H. W. Bush did not command the American troops to push ahead to Baghdad and remove Saddam from power. In a 1998 memoir entitled *A World Transformed*, the elder Bush wrote, "Trying to eliminate Saddam . . . would have incurred incalculable human and political costs."

When George W. Bush took office in 2001, Saddam Hussein was still in power in Iraq. After the Gulf War, Saddam rebuilt his army, reestablished his control of the nation and regained his reputation as the "bully" of the Middle East. Saddam demonstrated a sadistic and even maniacal tendency toward destruction by using chemical weapons and developing other weapons of mass destruction.

Following the 9/11 attacks on America, President Bush set out to diminish the threat of terror against the United States by attacking the strongholds of the terrorist group that caused the attacks—al Qaeda. He also began holding nations that aided terrorists accountable for their actions. Saddam Hussein once again proved unresponsive to United Nations requests for his cooperation, and the world suspected that he harbored weapons of mass destruction. The United States chose to stop this threat in the Middle East with offensive action, rather than staying on the defensive and waiting for another terrorist attack at home. Thus George W. Bush, the son, found himself pitted against Saddam Hussein, the nemesis of his father more than a decade before.

The United Nations demanded that Saddam disclose any weapons of mass destruction in his control or face military action. He refused to fully cooperate, and war was launched against Iraq by the United States, Britain and a few other allies in March 2003. One of the stated missions of this second war with Iraq was to end the reign of Saddam Hussein. Once again the American and allied forces routed the Iraqi army—at least initially. Baghdad fell within a month of the war's beginning, but the United States began a long occupation of Iraq that lasted more than eight years. George W. Bush's entire presidency would be defined by the War on Terror, including his invasion of Iraq.

The financial costs of this war were astronomical, with estimates ranging from slightly less than one trillion dollars to more than three trillion dollars. Yet the cost in human lives was much more significant, with more than 36,000 American men and women killed or wounded in battle. Beyond this, the war caused thousands of Iraqi military casualties and thousands of civilian casualties.

The father, George H. W. Bush, was correct in saying that removing Saddam would have "incalculable human and political costs." One must wonder, though, if those costs would not have been reduced had he taken a more aggressive approach during his time in office. During the Gulf War, only 2,500 American soldiers were killed or wounded. A stronger coalition existed, for international opinion sided with the United States. Saudi Arabia, along with other nations, helped fund Desert Storm. This would have been the best time to conclude the reign of Saddam Hussein, but the father was not willing to take the political risks. His son would reap the results of his unwillingness.

George W. Bush would have to finish what his father started by removing Saddam from power. In December 2003 Saddam Hussein was captured, and three years later, following a year-long trial in Iraq, was hanged for his crimes. One generation finished what the first generation would not. By the way, George H. W. Bush served only one term; George W. Bush served two! Compromise never works.

Finishing Off the Amalekites

The first king of Israel, Saul, was commanded to finish what Moses and Joshua began: Samuel instructed him to fulfill the judgment against the Amalekites recorded in Deuteronomy by completely destroying them. The prophet told Saul that the Lord had chosen him to be the instrument of punishment on the Amalekites for lying in wait for Israel as they came out of Egypt. The Lord said, "Do not spare them; put to death men and women, children and infants, cattle and sheep, camels and donkeys" (1 Samuel 15:3). Saul had a prophetic promise and a generational account to settle with the Amalekites.

King Saul attacked the Amalekites as God called him to do, and Israel won a great victory. Yet Saul was not completely obedient. Instead of destroying everything, he allowed the best of the Amalekite resources to be kept alive, and he also spared their king, Agag. Samuel, whom God used to instruct Saul in "Mission Amalekite Destruction," confronted Saul for his disobedience. Saul's explanation was that the people had kept the best of the Amalekite herds alive in order to sacrifice them to the Lord. Neither Samuel nor the Lord was impressed. Samuel answered, "To obey is better than sacrifice" (verse 22). He declared that because of Saul's disobedience in this generational battle against Amalek, "The LORD has torn the kingdom of Israel from you today and has given it to one of your neighbors—to one better than you" (verse 28).

Saul's compromise cost him his crown. Whatever keeps us from total obedience will also keep us from our destiny. Whatever causes us to compromise will someday take our crown, as it did for Saul.

Several years after the Amalekite disobedience, King Saul and his son Jonathan were at war with the Philistines near Mount Gilboa (1 Samuel 31–2 Samuel 1). The battle turned against Israel, and the Philistine army aggressively pursued them. The Philistines killed Jonathan and wounded Saul with an arrow. Realizing that he was crippled by his injuries and would be captured by his enemy, he decided it would be better to die than suffer humiliation and torture at the hands of the Philistines. Saul's armor bearer declined Saul's request to finish him, so Saul fell upon his own sword. The self-inflicted wound was not fatal, however; Saul remained alive, though mortally wounded. Something else or someone else would complete the story.

Saul lay wallowing in his own blood—shot by the Philistines, pierced by his own sword, yet still breathing. The

Philistines would soon arrive and Saul's worst nightmare would be realized. At that moment, a young man came up behind Saul. Saul asked him who he was, to which the young man answered, "I am an Amalekite." King Saul asked the young Amalekite to finish the job by standing on the sword until Saul's life was gone. The young man obliged him by ending the king's life and delivering the results of Saul's compromise. God's pattern remains: Sowing leads to reaping. Whatever makes you compromise will ultimately take your crown. Saul compromised with an Amalekite, and an Amalekite took his crown.

Later the young Amalekite rehearsed to David the story of how he helped Saul end his life, and then he gave David the crown that was on Saul's head. David had the young Amalekite executed for his crime against the king. David would not compromise with Amalek.

While Saul and Jonathan were losing their lives at Mount Gilboa, David, the next king, was facing one of his greatest challenges ever. His loosely knit band of guerillas returned to their temporary home in Ziklag to discover the Amalekites had invaded. They kidnapped and took captive their wives and children, stole their goods and set the encampment afire. As David and his men rode into Ziklag, smoke filled their nostrils, tears filled their eyes and anguish filled their hearts. David's men talked of stoning him because of the futile trip they had taken that allowed the Amalekites to once again attack vulnerable people.

David encouraged himself in the Lord, pursued the Amalekites and recovered everything the nomads had captured. While David was defeating the Amalekites, Saul was losing his crown to one. The defeat of the Amalekites was critical to David's ascension to the throne, while Saul's compromise with the Amalekites was critical to his descent from his destiny. The monarchy moved from the tribe of Benjamin to the tribe of Judah. David won the crown that Saul lost.

Leaving a Legacy

King Saul's children and grandchildren also lost: His children lost their lives, and his grandchildren lost their inheritance. They went from royalty to rejects because of the sins of their grandfather. The man chosen as the first king of Israel because of his humility brought reproach on multiple generations because of his prideful disobedience. It would take his family many years to recover.

God declares that He "does not leave the guilty unpunished; he punishes the children and their children for the sin of the parents to the third and fourth generation" (Exodus 34:7). In rightly dividing the Word of God, we must understand that this does not mean that I am held spiritually accountable before God for my father's or grandfather's sins. When I stand before God's throne, I will not answer for the works or failures of others, only for my own actions. This is obvious from other passages of Scripture, such as Ezekiel 18:20:

> The one who sins is the one who will die. The child will not share the guilt of the parent, nor will the parent share the guilt of the child. The righteousness of the righteous will be credited to them, and the wickedness of the wicked will be charged against them.

The results of that sin, however, will be experienced for several generations to come. Yet if our sins influence future generations, how much greater is the influence of righteousness on the future. The account of Jonathan

Edwards, one of the great spiritual leaders in American history, reveals this power of righteous living.

Edwards was a key figure in the First Great Awakening in America. While serving as a pastor in the New England village of Northampton, Edwards sought God consistently for revival. He wrote and preached until Northampton was swept into a great spiritual awakening that spread through the colonies. Edwards is perhaps most famous for his sermon "Sinners in the Hands of an Angry God." This sermon and others shook the American colonies for Christ. Edwards and his wife, Sarah, were stalwart believers who lived their faith, serving without compromise throughout their lives. The influence of their righteous living on future generations is astounding.

A study in the year 1900 followed the 1,400 descendants of Jonathan and Sarah Edwards and revealed that by the beginning of the twentieth century,

> this one marriage [had] produced 66 physicians, 30 judges, 65 professors, 13 college presidents, 100 lawyers, 1 Dean of the top law school, 1 Dean of a medical school, 3 US senators, 3 mayors of large cities, 3 state governors, 1 controller of the US Treasury, and 1 Vice-President of the USA—who the very next year became President of the USA—Theodore Roosevelt. In addition, members of the family had written 135 books and edited 18 journals. They had entered the ministry "*in platoons*" and sent out over 100 missionaries overseas.[1]

What a testimony and legacy!

A Crown for Queen Esther

Act one in the intergenerational battle with the Amalekites took place in the valley of Rephidim between Egypt and the Promised Land. Act two took place on the battlefields of Mount Gilboa and Ziklag. Act three will take us to the palace of the Persian kings (and queens) in a faraway place called Shushan.

The modern Iranian city of Shush is located where the great Babylonian and Persian capital of Shushan once stood. Assyrians, Babylonians and Persians all used the palaces built there. This was where Daniel lived and is buried. It also served as the backdrop for the biblical account of Esther.

As mentioned in the last chapter, Esther was orphaned at the death of her parents and adopted by her first cousin Mordecai, who became Esther's spiritual father, providing guidance and covering for her. God's favor on Esther's life brought her before the Persian king, Xerxes. Amazingly, this orphaned Jewish girl was selected to become the queen of Persia.

Esther and Mordecai came from the tribe of Benjamin; Mordecai was related to Kish, a Benjamite leader. Kish was also King Saul's father. Essentially, Mordecai and Esther were from the royal lineage of King Saul. Though Esther became queen of Persia, her generational connections must have reminded her of Israel. Undoubtedly Mordecai and Esther thought of the time when their most prominent relative, Saul (a man who was perhaps their several-times-over great-grandfather), was king of Israel. For the first time in generations, since the Amalekite lifted one from Saul's head at Mount Gilboa, a Benjamite from Saul's family was wearing a crown!

Another outsider lived in Shushan along with these Jews: Haman the Agagite, a relative of the Amalekite king saved by Saul in disobedience to God's command. Agag had cost Saul his crown. The unfolding plot of the book of Esther reveals that Haman, a relative of Agag, wanted to take the crown of Esther, a relative of Saul. The generation-to-generation conflict that began in the Sinai wilderness had traveled north to Shushan, with astounding effects. It took both Moses' generation and Joshua's generation working together to defeat Amalek in the Sinai wilderness, and it would take Mordecai's generation and Esther's generation working together to defeat Amalek in Persia.

Haman was promoted by Xerxes to a place of authority in the Persian government. Haman's position was so elevated that Persians bowed to him when he passed by them on the streets of Shushan. Actually, almost all of the people bowed, except for one. Mordecai refused to stoop to Haman, whose distant relative cost Mordecai's distant relative his crown. Mordecai would not compromise. Nor did he plan on losing the crown from the tribe of Benjamin this time.

Haman was furious that Mordecai the Jew would not bow, so he devised a plan to destroy all the Jews. He also built a seven-story gallows on which he planned to punish Mordecai by hanging. Haman offered Xerxes the equivalent of more than 400 billion dollars in today's currency to implement his genocidal plan. Xerxes agreed to Haman's offer, the decree was signed and the Jewish people were to be eradicated.

Upon hearing about Haman's "Jewish Solution," Mordecai cried out, tore his garment and declared a fast. He was broken before God and was bold before Queen Esther. He challenged Esther with the thought of destiny. Spiritual fathers should always speak destiny to their spiritual children. Mordecai did this to Esther at this critical moment; he reminded her that God had positioned her as queen, and she had come into the kingdom "for such a time as this."

Mordecai also warned Esther that if she failed to get involved in the situation, her Jewish roots would be discovered, and she, too, would be killed even though she was living in the king's palace. Esther responded courageously by asking Mordecai and the people to fast with her for three days before she approached King Xerxes. While Mordecai and the Jews went before God with fasting, Esther went before the king with favor. She risked everything by approaching the king without first being called, which could have easily meant her execution. Thankfully, instead of anger she obtained access.

Esther showed great wisdom and restraint with Xerxes, waiting until precisely the right moment to present her request for the king to help her people, the Jews. Esther identified herself as a Jewish queen for the first time. She did not hold back. She did not play political games. She did not compromise because of her fear. Xerxes was touched and asked Esther who in the world would want to destroy her people. Esther could have told the ancient stories of multiple generations being attacked and hated by the Amalekites, but instead she just pointed to Haman.

Haman feared for his life, and with good reason. Xerxes ultimately commanded that Haman be hanged on the gallows he had built for Mordecai for all of Persia to see. A new decree was written, allowing the Jews to defend themselves against Haman's "Jewish Solution," and the people of God were saved. Mordecai was exalted, Haman was abased and Esther kept her crown. The Amalekite attack was foiled by generations working together and placing their trust in the Lord.

In Moses and Joshua's battle against the Amalekites, intercession and action worked together. The same was true in Persia. Fasting and prayer were required for the invisible battle in the heavenlies, and bold action was required for the visible battle on earth. The failure of Saul in his compromise with Agag was not repeated; Mordecai and Esther restored honor to the tribe of Benjamin and demonstrated their true royal bloodline. They were able to take back what past generations had relinquished.

In many ways the victory of Mordecai and Esther in Persia was a reclamation of what was lost in the compromise of their relative, King Saul, with the Amalekites. Saul lost a crown. Esther and Mordecai retained one. Saul kept alive that which was an enemy to God. Esther and Mordecai saw God's enemies destroyed. What one generation loses, another can regain.

If your spiritual father has fallen, you do not have to. If you come from a family of alcoholics, you do not have to become an alcoholic. If your parents are divorced, you still can have a great marriage. If fathers or mothers—whether spiritual or physical—compromised and lost their crowns, you do not have to lose yours. Together spiritual fathers and mothers and spiritual sons and daughters can bring down the generational enemies we fight in the twenty-first century. With consistent intercession and courageous engagement, we can stand on the battlefield of our times and proclaim victory from generation to generation.

5

Spiritual Parents Needed Now!

Even if you had ten thousand guardians in Christ,
you do not have many fathers, for in Christ Jesus
I became your father through the gospel.

1 Corinthians 4:15

The cry from this generation for spiritual fathers and mothers is a cry for spiritual survival amidst death. Today's young person endures a level of spiritual warfare and attack beyond anything any age group has ever experienced. Twenty-four hours a day, seven days a week, people now coming of age are pummeled with images of impurity, violence, anger, murder, deceit and death. The level of this assault is unprecedented.

Although I believe completely in the power of Christ's Kingdom in the present age and the hope His Kingdom brings to the broken, I also understand that God's Word predicts social deterioration as we near the second coming of Jesus:

But mark this: There will be terrible times in the last days. People will be lovers of themselves, lovers of money, boastful, proud, abusive, disobedient to their parents, ungrateful, unholy, without love, unforgiving, slanderous, without self-control, brutal, not lovers of the good, treacherous, rash, conceited, lovers of pleasure rather than lovers of God—having a form of godliness but denying its power. Have nothing to do with such people.

2 Timothy 3:1–5

Proverbs also describes the generation that continues in moral deterioration:

There are those who curse their fathers and do not bless their mothers; those who are pure in their own eyes and yet are not cleansed of their filth; those whose eyes are ever so haughty, whose glances are so disdainful; those whose teeth are swords and whose jaws are set with knives to devour the poor from the earth and the needy from among mankind.

Proverbs 30:11–14

The days in which we are walking are referred to in Scripture, and we are witnessing foundational erosion on a broad scale. Postmodernity has brought the collapse of certainty and with it a collapse of morality. This collapse has created a very confusing scenario for today's youth, where nothing seems dependable or eternal. Self has become god, and one's personal opinion about matters has become doctrine. Biblical illiteracy is up, moral certainty is down. Our world rushes headlong into the night, and the spiritual darkness is enveloping millions of young people today. It is like the darkness mentioned in Egypt during the deliverance of Israel from bondage; it is a "darkness that can be felt."

Several years ago my wife, Lisa, and I visited and took the obligatory tour of a cave in our area of Tennessee. Inside the cave we descended with a small group to a large underground room. Following our descent the guide stated, "Make sure you are standing firm and please do not move. It is about to get very dark." Was that an understatement! The lights were turned off, and it was *dark*! I mean the complete, "no light at all" kind of dark. It was a darkness that could be felt. Whether I closed my eyes or opened them did not matter; I could not see anything. Lisa moved closer and clutched my arm. Just knowing someone was there amidst the darkness seemed to help.

More recently I happily endured an outing with my grandchildren to Disney World. We had a great day punctuated by numerous fun moments and a few scary ones. On one of the roller coaster rides, my granddaughter Anna sat beside me. The ride was fast, the turns were scary and it was dark part of the way. Anna clung to me continually. By the time we were finished, I thought I would have to pry her hands off my arm with a crowbar. Just having someone with her that she could depend on made the ride bearable and the darkness less scary.

This generation of young men and women is looking for people they can trust amid the darkness. They need people who are not afraid and who will not run when things get scary. Their ride through life has more vicious curves than they expected, and things are going much faster than their minds can fathom. Is there an anchor? Is there anyone they can trust? Is there a way to get to the end without losing it?

Following the Empowered21 Global Congress in Tulsa, we decided to survey some of its participants regarding spiritual fathers and mothers to determine their views on what qualities are most important in the people who fill these roles in their life. Among those surveyed, 83 percent felt spiritual parenting was critical for new generations. They said that the three most important qualities for spiritual fathers and mothers to possess were spiritual integrity, spiritual maturity and trustworthiness/faithfulness. They did not choose giftedness or ability or passion, which were also on the list. The good news for those who want to serve and help "parent" this generation is that you do not have to be good looking, you do not have to have charisma, and you do not even have to be overly knowledgeable to be a spiritual parent. You do, however, need to be faithful, have integrity and be mature enough to stand tall amidst the darkness. Young men and women today should be able to cling tightly to someone they can trust through this wild ride called life.

One other vital quality for a spiritual parent in this culture of death is spiritual power or life. Only those who have enough spiritual life to not only sustain themselves but give it away to others can help raise this generation up to fulfill its destiny.

We see this power demonstrated in Elisha, who accomplished his journey from spiritual child to spiritual parent after Elijah's departure to heaven in a whirlwind. He took up Elijah's mantle and began his prophetic ministry in a time of continuing moral darkness. The influence of Jezebel and Ahab was still present. The worship of pagan deities like Baal was interwoven into the everyday lives of the Israelite people, and the darkness seemed impenetrable. In this "darkness that could be felt" scenario, God used Elisha to break the oppression and turn many in Israel back to the living God.

Elisha's itinerate teaching ministry carried him throughout the nation of Israel. One of the places he frequented was a small village in northern Israel, in the area named Shunem, once assigned to the tribe of Issachar. While in Shunem, Elisha visited consistently with a renowned woman and her husband (see 2 Kings 4). She entertained Elisha and his servant, feeding them each time they were in town. The woman eventually talked her husband into doing more than just hosting Elisha and his servant for a meal; she convinced him to make an extra room attached to their home where Elisha could stay when visiting in Shunem. Furnished with a bed, a table, a stool and a candlestick, these "prophet quarters" would be a place of study and rest for the man of God.

Elisha, blessed by this significant gesture of generosity and full of gratitude, wanted to do something to thank the Shunammite and her husband for their gracious care. He called for the woman and offered to use his clout politically or militarily on her behalf. She refused the offer, stating that she was satisfied to dwell in the small village of Shunem without any special favors from the well-intentioned prophet.

Gehazi, Elisha's servant, then mentioned that the Shunammite woman did not have a child, although she and her husband were old. Elisha called for her again and announced that she was going to have a son within a year. Elisha's prophetic word was fulfilled, and the generous, elderly couple welcomed a bouncing baby boy into their home. What a gift from God! What a delight to hold the product of God's promise in their own arms! Elisha watched the baby grow, and every time he went to Shunem, he rejoiced in God's blessing on this family that had blessed him so much. Their child was born from a promise. He was born with a destiny and without doubt was being groomed for greatness. For many years after that, all went well.

When the young lad was old enough to learn how to harvest, he joined his father, who was working with the reapers in the field. The son of promise suffered an attack in his brain while harvesting and began to cry out because of the pain. We are not sure if the boy had an aneurysm or if he suffered a heat stroke in the Middle Eastern sun. His father sent the boy home to his mother. When the lad arrived, he laid his head in his mother's lap for a few hours and died. During a time of harvest—a time of hope—this young man died following an attack to his head. The progeny of promise descended into the depths of death right in the house of hope.

This is an accurate description of many young people today who are under severe mental attack and are dying before our very eyes in God's house of hope—the Church. The young men and women who serve Jesus in today's Church are a generation of promise. God has given them to us in answer to the prayers of the last two thousand years, and they have a destiny. They have been born into the greatest time of Christian harvest in history. They are gifted and smart and have a prophetic purpose. The harvest potential surrounding us means they are needed now more than ever.

A Vast Harvest Field

More than seven billion people inhabit the world. In *The World Factbook* the Central Intelligence Agency estimates that by July 2012, approximately 107 people will die each minute.[1] This would result in 56.2 million deaths per year, an average of more than 154,000 each day. If one-third of these people are Christian[2]—which is a generous estimate—each day 102,720 people will go into eternity in

2012 without knowing Jesus Christ as their Savior. That means 4,280 people each hour, 71 people every minute or more than one person every second are entering eternal darkness and punishment. With 37.5 million people each year descending into a Christ-less eternity, the Scripture is certainly being fulfilled that "hell hath enlarged herself" (Isaiah 5:14, KJV).

Added to the weight of our eternal burden for those who are dying is the even greater burden for those who are living. The 2012 estimated births are more than 132 million.[3] With 362,880 babies born each day—15,120 an hour, 252 each minute and 4.2 every second—the population explosion of our time continues. By 2025 the earth's population will exceed 8 billion.[4] This means that if we in today's Church do our job well and bring our generation to Christ, potentially more people could be in heaven from this generation than from other generations combined. Today's young person has the potential to be one of the chief instruments God uses to preach the Gospel and disciple people for Christ. They are positioned to reap the greatest harvest in human history.

The prince of darkness, Satan, knows this and would attack this generation in their heads (like the Shunammite's son) before they ever do damage to his domain. Lucifer's attack on the minds of today's youth is multifaceted; things like pluralism, pornography, poor self-image and powerless churches combine to keep their minds off their purpose. His instruments of attack include everything from media to moral failure in the lives of those they trust.

A few years ago I counseled a young man whose life graphically demonstrated the level of this attack. Super-intelligent and sharp-looking, this man had a great personality and was easily recognized as a leader. He felt called to ministry, and his potential was astounding. He married a wonderful young lady and quickly had two beautiful children. The circumstances were ideal: I would have predicted that this young man would ascend quickly in whatever area he chose to pursue. It excited me because I thought he would continue in ministry, and I felt certain he would be a great harvester for Christ. Satan's kingdom, I believed, was in jeopardy because of this son of promise.

I had every reason to continue in this hope until a counseling visit in my office one difficult afternoon revealed the deep struggle in this young man's heart and the monstrous attack going on in his head. He was depressed and felt down on himself. I tried to encourage him, but I suddenly discerned that something besides just discouragement was going on. At that moment he began to share his deep struggle with homosexuality. He had fallen multiple times and needed forgiveness. We prayed together. He repented and I hoped for the best. Ultimately my hopes were dashed—at least up to this point. His continual failure with the sin of homosexuality would cost him his family, his church positions, his ministry and his relationship with God. A potential harvester descended into death and darkness before my very eyes.

During our times of counseling he shared how he had become trapped in this sin. Had he been abused? No. Did he feel this way early in life? No. Were his feelings for men caused by genetics? Absolutely not! What pushed him into this addiction and lifestyle? When he came to college, he was a pure young man; he was serving the Lord and excited about a future in ministry. One night he made one too many clicks while he was on the Internet. Just one click! He found himself at a website containing homosexual pornography, and his mind was drawn in. His interest and lusts were heightened. He had opened the wrong tab and entered a door that continues to entrap him until this day. As he rattled off the horror of his sexual escapades with multiple partners, I was shaken and sickened. To be honest, by the time he was finished I felt like I needed a spiritual shower to cleanse this stuff from my mind. I was amazed at how much damage one click could do to a person's mind and soul. How could such great potential die so quickly?

Power to Bring Life

The Shunammite mother must have been asking the same question when she held her dead son of promise. The child of her old age, the delight of her heart, was gone. What would she—what *could* she—possibly do? Quickly she took the boy's corpse into Elisha's "Prophet Quarters"— the place where the prophet had given her the prophetic promise—and put him on the prophet's bed. She returned to where God had spoken to her. She went back to God's place of promise.

Sometimes when our sight does not match our faith, we need to return to the place of promise where we can regain our footing on the rock of God's character. This was one of those moments. God promised a son and delivered. Her boy had died, and the promise seemed dead with him. God must have something in mind because He does not lie. It was not time for a funeral. It was time for faith. The Shunammite may have remembered the time another young man had died during the ministry of Elijah, Elisha's spiritual father.

According to 1 Kings 17, Elijah was taking refuge at the house of a widow and her son in Zarephath during the severe three-and-a-half-year Israelite drought. Every day was a miracle as the widow discovered enough meal and oil to cook for the trio, despite the fact her supply should have been depleted months earlier. One day the son of the woman became sick and suddenly died. Death in the midst of miracles simply does not make sense. Her only companion, her only son, was dead despite God's miraculous supply. She had been generous, and now her son was gone. At the moment of confusion and distress, Elijah took the young man's corpse in his arms, putting him on his own bed in the widow's house. Eventually, God raised him to life through Elijah. Perhaps the Shunammite woman knew this account and emulated it when she brought the corpse of her son to Elisha's room.

After carefully placing the dead promise on the prophet's pallet, she rode quickly to find Elisha. Following several hours of travel by donkey between Shunem and Mount Carmel, the grieving mother came near to where Elisha and Gehazi were staying. Gehazi ran out to see if she was well, questioning her about herself, her husband and her son. Was something wrong? She merely answered, "It is well" (2 Kings 4:26, KJV). She maintained her spiritual composure despite her loss and pain. Gehazi took her to Elisha, before whom she broke with emotion, falling down at Elisha's feet in bitter distress. When Elisha heard the story of the young boy's death and the fact that the corpse of the lad was lying on his bed, he reacted quickly.

Elisha sent Gehazi with his staff to the Shunammite's house while he followed with her to see what God would do. When Gehazi placed the prophet's staff on the corpse, nothing happened. The depth of this death could not be conquered with long-distance ministry or symbolic gestures of spiritual authority. Some things simply require personal engagement and involvement. The attack on this generation and the culture of death surrounding them is one of those things. We cannot bring life to today's young men and women with long-distance ministry; we must get involved with them. They need us to personally connect and bring them life.

When Elisha arrived at the Shunammite's home, it must have been startling. The young boy, whom Elisha saw playing around the house only months earlier, lay lifeless in his room. What would he do? What do spiritual fathers do when their spiritual sons or daughters have been attacked by darkness and lie in spiritual death? We raise the dead!

Elisha may have thought back to his spiritual father, Elijah. Elisha was now a spiritual father, and he was facing a similar situation as one previously faced by his spiritual father. What would Elijah do in this situation? What did he do? In every generation, spiritual sons and daughters must face the challenges of their day, which will be very similar to those faced by their spiritual fathers and those who have gone before them. The way we handle those challenges will determine whether life or death is victorious in future generations.

In 1 Kings 17, the account of the widow of Zarephath's son dying is punctuated with the story of God's power at work in Elijah's ministry. Elijah cried out to God and stretched himself on the corpse three times in prayer, asking the Lord to allow the soul of the young man to return. We read in 1 Kings 17:22, "The LORD heard Elijah's cry, and the boy's life returned to him, and he lived."

Elisha, the new spiritual father, may have mentally referred to Elijah's method of bringing the dead to life because he also stretched himself on the corpse of the Shunammite lad. He put his eyes on the young man's eyes, his mouth on the boy's mouth and his hands on the corpse's hands. Seemingly Elisha tried a type of resuscitation in order to bring the boy back to the land of the living. When Elisha stretched himself out on the boy initially, the boy's body warmed, but no other sign of life was evident. Elisha walked back and forth in the room. Personally I believe Elisha met with God in prayer and a faith-building moment happened as he walked around, because at the end of it, Elisha returned to stretch himself on the corpse once more. Once again he placed his body eye to eye, mouth to mouth and hand to hand. This time something happened: Life came back into the young man. The boy sneezed seven times and sat up—alive! Elisha had raised the dead just like his spiritual father before him. The Shunammite mother was elated that God's promise is sure even when death tries to negate it.

Elisha demonstrated a principle that I believe is critical for spiritual fathers and mothers in our day. It is the principle of life. If we are to raise a new generation of Christ followers from the culture of death in which we live, we must have enough spiritual power and life to raise the dead. Spiritual parents must have enough spiritual life to keep themselves in the faith along with enough life to help someone else. Elisha was so full of spiritual life that even after his own death, the corpse of a man resurrected when it touched his bones in a burial cave (2 Kings 13:21). We need to be so full of spiritual power and spiritual life that even years after our death, the testimony of our walk with Jesus will bring life to new generations.

Every group of spiritual fathers and mothers must pass this "life" test. Do we have what it takes to resurrect today's youth into new life? This is the true test of a spiritual parent. The apostle Paul passed the test; how about you?

Do More Than Just Preach

In Acts 20, we read of Paul preaching to the Christians of Troas, a city which had served as a launching point for ministry in Europe years before. On this Sunday evening, he preached a *long* time. We may be preaching the everlasting Gospel, but this does not mean our preaching should be everlasting. One of my spiritual fathers commented regarding the length of a message, "If, after twenty minutes, you don't strike oil, quit boring." I have never heard a sermon that I could follow for two or three hours, and Paul's sermon in Troas probably lasted longer. When midnight came, Paul was still preaching, and he kept sermonizing into the night.

Even someone as interesting as Paul can overdo it and become boring to even the most engaged listener. A young man named Eutychus was sitting in the window of the church, listening to the apostle preach on and on. It is notable that Eutychus was in the window. He was sort of in the church and sort of out of it. He could hear what was transpiring inside, and he could hear what was happening outside. He could see the world and the church at the same time, and he was somewhere in between. The combination of boring preachers, increasing darkness and a lack of commitment spell trouble for young people. Eutychus fell into a deep sleep, and it became clear that he was leaning the wrong way: He fell out of the window. The three-story fall ended in the tragedy of Eutychus's death. Paul's marathon message was interrupted by a literal falling out. What would the great apostle do? What should any true spiritual parent do when a young person has fallen away and is enveloped in death? We should raise the dead!

Paul stopped preaching. He moved from long-distance ministry to personal connection. The great apostle quickly found the lifeless corpse of Eutychus on the ground outside the window and threw himself on it. Paul wrapped his arms around Eutychus's lifeless form, and God raised the young man from the dead.

> Seated in a window was a young man named Eutychus, who was sinking into a deep sleep as Paul talked on and on. When he was sound asleep, he fell to the ground from the third story and was picked up dead. Paul went down, threw himself on the young man and put his arms around him. "Don't be alarmed," he said. "He's alive!"
>
> Acts 20:9–10

Paul's tactic in raising a dead person from the younger generation was similar to that of Elijah and Elisha. It involved personal connection and spiritual power.

For those of us who are called to be spiritual fathers and mothers to new generations, the one quality we must possess above all others is spiritual life—spiritual power that will not only keep us alive when death is all around us but also allow us to share spiritual life with a new generation under mental attack from a culture of death. Someone shared God's grace and life with you in the past. Someone was your spiritual father or mother. Someone now needs you to embrace them and share the life of Jesus. A new generation must be raised to reap the harvest before us. Are you willing to personally connect with young men and women from another generation? Will you stand against the darkness and raise the dead in the face of this culture of death? Do you have what it takes? If so, you qualify to be a spiritual parent.

6

Sons and Daughters Wanted

To Timothy my true son in the faith . . .

1 Timothy 1:2

Elisha saw this and cried out, "My father! My father! The chariots and horsemen of Israel!" And Elisha saw him no more.

2 Kings 2:12

Are you kidding me? This must have been Timothy's reaction when the apostle Paul relayed the prerequisite for joining his ministry team. Perhaps his grandmother and mother reacted similarly, though they probably understood Paul's reasoning better than young Timothy. Timothy was undoubtedly excited that such a great leader was showing so much confidence in him. He had been chosen to participate in the inner circle of Paul's team. What a thrill this must have been for a young believer like Timothy. Any young man or woman will respond positively to personal affirmation.

Timothy was also excited about the possibilities of traveling, of sharing the message of Jesus with those who had never heard and of witnessing firsthand the power of God in Paul's ministry. The first requirement for this promotion, however, seemed a bit extreme, especially to Timothy. Paul wanted Timothy, now a young adult, to be circumcised! Becoming the spiritual son of the great apostle had its price.

I suspect that if we told young adult Christian males the prerequisite for entry into ministry was a crude operation on their private parts without anesthesia, performed by a preacher rather than a surgeon, the number of ministerial applicants would fall to an all-time low. Yet this is exactly what Paul required. Timothy was born into a multifaith home. His mother, Eunice, was a Christian believer from a Jewish background, and his father was a Gentile, a polytheistic Greek. As a result Timothy had not been circumcised according to Jewish custom as a child, and he found himself now facing the painful embarrassment of the adult version of foreskin removal. Luke records this moment in Timothy's life:

> Paul came to Derbe and then to Lystra, where a disciple named Timothy lived, whose mother was Jewish and a believer but whose father was a Greek. The believers at Lystra and Iconium spoke well of him. Paul wanted to take him along on the journey, so he circumcised him because of the Jews who lived in that area, for they all knew that his father was a Greek.
>
> Acts 16:1–3

One should note that Paul was fresh from the Jerusalem council (recorded in Acts 15), during which the Church leadership made a critical decision for the advancement of the Gospel. A controversy among Christian believers with a Jewish background and the Gentile Christian believers had been brewing for several years. At the center of the division lay the requirements for a person who received Christ as their Savior. As the Church grew, this question also grew: Should converted Gentiles come under the physical sign of God's covenant with Abraham, which was circumcision? Should a non-Hebrew believer become a Jew in his flesh along with becoming a Christian in his heart?

The answer from the elders who met in Jerusalem to discuss this matter was no. Male Gentile converts did not need to endure adult or child circumcision. This outward sign of God's covenant with Abraham was not necessary for acceptance in the Body of Christ. When Paul arrived at the Lystra/Derbe area where Timothy lived, he was beginning a ministry trip to tell Gentile believers about the wonderful consolation the Church was giving them: Circumcision would not be required. Undoubtedly this was a great time of rejoicing among the Gentile Christians, especially the men!

Yet Paul would require Timothy to endure this extremely painful and personal process before taking him into his ministry circle. Timothy would need to be circumcised before going to tell the Gentiles they did not have to be circumcised. Timothy was required to allow the most private areas of his life to be revealed and cut by the person who would become his spiritual father. Timothy became vulnerable for the sake of the Gospel. These were Timothy's first conscious steps toward spiritual sonship.

One of the issues we have continued to encounter globally regarding the father cry of this generation is not only the lack of spiritual fathers and mothers but also the lack of spiritual sons and daughters. Pastors, leaders and youth workers around the world struggle at times to find people who are willing to step up and carry God's torch into the twenty-first century. Plenty of young people love Jesus and desire to serve Him, but far fewer are willing to pay the price to position themselves for true promotion in God's Kingdom.

What does it mean to be a spiritual son or daughter? What are the requirements? What steps should young people take to position themselves for Kingdom advancement and the fulfilling of God's purposes in their lives? I personally believe millions of Christian young people want spiritual fathers and mothers; they just do not know what their roles should be in this relationship.

The Empowered21 survey we conducted following the 2010 Empowered21 Global Congress included some of these questions.[1] We asked the respondents for the most important qualities spiritual sons and daughters should possess. The answers they gave encouraged me and should encourage you if you are a young person reading this book. In a list of ten qualities, the top three chosen were (1) teachable, (2) having spiritual hunger and desire and (3) able to receive counsel and instruction. Close behind these top three qualities were faithfulness and accountability.

The other choices on the list included giftedness and talent, potential, ability to work with another generation and various other skills. Some of these qualities, which are typically considered of higher value, were ranked at the bottom. In fact, natural giftedness or ability was the lowest-ranked quality that those surveyed felt spiritual sons and daughters needed to possess. This is very important for our understanding, and I believe it also agrees with Scripture. A person does not have to be smart or talented or have lots of potential to be a good spiritual son or daughter; they must, however, be teachable, faithful and pliable, demonstrating significant hunger for God.

When Paul arrived at Derbe and Lystra, he discovered that Timothy had these most important qualities. Luke relates that the elders of the churches spoke well of Timothy (Acts 16:2). Timothy was timid and perhaps even a bit backward, but he had proven himself to the church leaders. He was faithful. He would not run when ministry got tough the way John Mark abandoned Paul's team, as recorded in Acts 15:38. Paul needed someone he could trust. He was going to the regions beyond those in which he had already ministered, where the attacks of darkness would escalate to life-threatening levels. He needed someone who was faithful, he needed someone who could make a commitment and he needed someone who would not shrink back from pain. Timothy's first test was the pain and commitment of circumcision. As painful as it was, he passed the test.

One basis for every intergenerational mentoring relationship in Scripture is the willingness of the mentee to make a significant commitment. Joshua risked his life in war with the Amalekites. Ruth left her homeland of Moab for Bethlehem, never to return. Elisha killed his oxen and used his plow for firewood, breaking the tie to his previous means of employment. Esther risked her life to request an appointment with the king. Timothy endured circumcision. Commitment is a must—it is critical to the relationship between spiritual parents and spiritual children. Without a strong commitment to each other and to God's plan in the relationship, it is impossible for long-term intergenerational mentoring to occur. The young person requiring this kind of commitment from the older must realize that the older person also needs similar assurance from the young.

Timothy's commitment to Paul was solid throughout the years. From the circumcision moment at Derbe and Lystra to Paul's summoning Timothy to his jail cell in Rome at the end of his life, Timothy was committed.

Commitment is one of the things with which this generation of young adults struggles the most. Much has been said about young adults' "failure to launch" tendencies. An article by Robin Marantz Henig, published in the *New York Times Sunday Magazine*, addressed the trend among "20-Somethings" to mature slower than other generations have through the years.[2] Henig charted numerous signs of this extended adolescence, or *emerging adulthood*, as it is called: One-third of young adults in their twenties move to a new residence each year, while 40 percent move back into their parents' homes at least once. Members of this unique group go through an average of seven jobs while in their twenties. Marriage is also occurring later than ever: The median ages for getting married among baby boomers in the early 1970s were 21 for women and 23 for men. By 2009 they had climbed to 26 for women and 28 for men—a five-year increase in slightly more than one generation.[3]

Sociologists usually describe five markers, or milestones, that people accomplish as they move from adolescence to adulthood: completing school, leaving home, becoming financially independent, marrying and having a child. In 1960, 77 percent of women and 65 percent of men had passed all five milestones by the time they reached age 30. Among 30-year-olds in the year 2000, according to the United States Census Bureau, fewer than 50 percent of the women and 33 percent of the men had completed the five milestones.[4]

Overall, this group of emerging adults seems more than five years behind where the last generation was in their

sociological development at the same age. One result of
this is an aversion to any commitment that is long term
or might require pain. This has left ministries and church
leaders scratching their heads and asking how they can
possibly prepare this generation for leadership when they
are not willing to make a commitment. Paul understood,
and so should we, that this is simply not possible.

The Model Spiritual Son

Elijah also understood this principle. Following God's
instruction, he recruited Elisha to serve as prophet in his
place. When the elder prophet touched the plough boy
with his mantle, or cloak, Elisha immediately responded.
Leaving his oxen, he ran after Elijah and asked if he could
tell his parents good-bye before joining the prophet. Elisha went home, killed his oxen, burned up his plow, said
farewell to his parents and rushed into his prophetic destiny. Elisha became Elijah's servant for many years, during
which he "poured water on the hands of Elijah" (2 Kings
3:11, KJV).

The Jews were taught under the Law to wash their hands
ritualistically. They were also taught to wash them prac-
tically before eating food and after using the bathroom.
We must remember that in Elijah's day, toilet paper did
not exist. In many Eastern nations, people still use their
hands to clean themselves after evacuation. This means that
Elijah's spiritual son was with him in intimate moments
when he needed excrement cleansed from his hands. Elisha
knew Elijah's humanness while also seeing God's power
rest upon him. Washing someone's hands, especially given
the grungy details, was not the most glamorous job. Elisha
went from being a plough boy to being a water boy. He

served Elijah in this way for a period between seven and twenty years. Elisha was committed.

Elisha also exhibited the kind of spiritual hunger required to be a good spiritual son or daughter. When Elijah was preparing for his high-speed earth-to-heaven excursion in a chariot of fire, he told Elisha to leave him and remain behind. Elisha refused, demonstrating what I like to call "spiritual savvy." I always look for this quality when recruiting a young person into our ministry. It is rare, but it is necessary for spiritual sons and daughters.

In 2 Kings 2, we read the details of Elijah and Elisha's intergenerational journey, which took them through places that both recalled God's dealings with Israel and revealed critical aspects of the spiritual father-son relationship. Their starting point at Gilgal was the place where a younger generation of Israelites, coming out of their sojourn in the wilderness, was circumcised before moving on to conquer Jericho and the Promised Land. Elisha stayed with Elijah through this juncture. Like Timothy, every spiritual son must be willing to make a circumcision-like commitment.

Elisha remained with Elijah when he moved on to Bethel. In this place, Jacob received a vision of a ladder reaching into the heavens, with angels ascending and descending. He called the place *Bethel*, which means "the house of God." When a spiritual son or daughter is faithful to a spiritual parent, the two will be able to be together in places of supernatural visitation. They will know not only the pain of commitment but also experience the joy of God's presence.

The third stop on Elijah's commute to eternity was Jericho, and Elisha was still with him. This was spiritual savvy on display. Jericho is the place where the people of God saw their faith activated to win the victory. This was a place of long-remembered, exemplary triumph. One of the things mentors pour into those they shepherd are their memories of victory, thus inspiring new generations with God's ability to keep His promises. Some of the greatest memories I have of my mentors are in this area. When they rehearsed the victories God gave them in their lives, they inspired me to believe. Any trip to Jericho would surely do the same.

The fourth stop for Elijah and Elisha was the river Jordan, where Elijah would part the waters by smiting them with his cloak. Elisha would follow this example after Elijah's departure. Elisha learned that he could witness God's power to make a way where there seems to be no way. His mentor not only taught him God had given victory in the past but also that God would open the future to him if he would just believe and move in faith.

At every stop Elisha was discouraged by Elijah, and at times by others, from continuing on this journey. Yet Elisha was persistent. He was spiritually hungry for more of God and wanted more than anything else to be identified as Elijah's spiritual son. Just before Elijah's departure, Elisha asked for a double portion of the Spirit that was on Elijah. In the Eastern world, a double portion was the amount of inheritance reserved for the firstborn. In essence Elisha was saying, "I want the firstborn portion of blessing from you as my spiritual father." He received it!

Elisha was present when Elijah departed. He picked up Elijah's fallen mantle and carried it until his own death. This mantle on a new generation represented an increased anointing and double-portion grace. Elisha performed twice as many miracles as Elijah and was used of God to do things Elijah only dreamed about doing—including witnessing the demise of Jezebel and of Ahab's line. Elisha was a more stable leader than Elijah and found a portion of strength that seemed to elude his fiery predecessor. Elisha was humble, he was teachable, he was spiritually hungry, he could receive counsel, he was faithful, he was accountable and he was committed. Elisha was a good spiritual son. Because of this he became a spiritual father in Israel, who without doubt wanted to mentor someone that could carry the prophetic mantle into a new generation.

Where Is the Successor?

It is disappointing that the chain of spiritual parenthood and spiritual sonship that began with Elijah and Elisha would so quickly be interrupted. First came Elijah, then came Elisha, then came . . . ? Though Elisha became a spiritual father throughout Israel, at the end of his life, he had not passed the cloak of prophetic leadership to a spiritual son. There was a prophetic discontinuation following Elisha's ministry, and he took his anointing to his grave. Why? Why did Elisha fail to pass the mantle the way it was passed to him? The answer seems to be that no spiritual son qualified for the assignment. Elisha actually seemed to have two or three potential successors for his ministry, but all of them were disqualified in some way before they took up the mantle.

Elisha's natural successor would have been the person who was serving him the way he had served Elijah. Elisha's servant Gehazi is mentioned first in the story of the Shunammite woman whose son was resurrected. Though we only see a brief picture of Gehazi, we can note he was faithful to Elisha and willing to serve him in any way possible. You would think that as a firsthand witness of Elisha's double-portion anointing, Gehazi would have a growing spiritual desire similar to Elisha's growing hunger as he traveled with Elijah. Elisha's ministry was filled with the miraculous, and Gehazi was a participant with him. Most people would have expected the anointing that rested first on Elijah and then on Elisha to someday rest on Gehazi. They would have been disappointed.

In 2 Kings 5, we read the account of Naaman, a Syrian army captain, being healed of leprosy under Elisha's ministry. While still dripping from his seven dips in the Jordan River, Naaman came to Elisha to give an offering for his miraculous healing. With his leprosy gone, Naaman was rejoicing and wanted to bless the man of God, who had been used to bless him. This was understandable and probably even appropriate; Elisha, however, refused to accept Naaman's offer. God's blessing and healing power are more than money could ever buy, and Elisha wanted to make sure that Naaman understood this.

Gehazi thought differently. If a Gentile captain wanted to share the riches of Syria with a Jewish prophet, they should not disappoint him, nor allow their own pockets to remain empty. When Naaman left Elisha, Gehazi secretly followed and talked Naaman into giving his proposed offering to him, which the servant would keep for his own. Naaman was generous, Gehazi was greedy and Elisha was frustrated. Gehazi quickly hid the treasure he received and returned to Elisha, claiming that he had not gone anywhere. Elisha discerned what Gehazi had done and knew his own servant had taken advantage of the situation for personal gain. Elisha told Gehazi that the leprosy Naaman left in the Jordan River would now cleave to Gehazi, and the generations that followed him would also be leprous. Gehazi was disqualified from his own double portion because of his greed, his deceptive heart and his failure to honor his spiritual father. Instead of a life filled with anointing, he received a life filled with alienation.

Another person who might have carried the mantle into a new generation was a young captain in the Israelite army. Having been anointed with a special package of oil from Elisha, Jehu was moved by the anointing of God to bring down Jezebel and Ahab's house along with Baal worship in Israel. Jehu was used of God mightily under the released anointing of Elisha. God's presence on him would have made him a logical candidate to carry the mantle.

Although Jehu was inspired and used by God, he was not a finisher. After becoming king he refused to dismantle the religious structures at Dan and Bethel that kept God's people from the Temple in Jerusalem. According to 2 Kings 10:31 (KJV), Jehu "took no heed to walk in the law of the LORD God of Israel with all his heart." Jehu was great on the big stage of life, bringing down Jezebel, Ahab's sons and the priests of Baal. He was not so great, however, at keeping his own heart right before God. Jehu was disqualified because of his failure to finish well and his unwillingness to make things right even when doing so might prove painful. His character did not match his charisma.

During the last days of Elisha's life, a third person appeared to have the potential for carrying the cloak of God into a new generation. By the time of his audition, recorded in 2 Kings 13, Elisha was on his deathbed. He was an old man who had served the Lord fully. His days of miraculous proclamation had ended, and he was now confined to bed, awaiting God's call to join his spiritual father, Elijah, in heaven. The mantle—the precious mantle—he had picked up years before near the Jordan River may have lain by his side, or perhaps he was wearing it despite his feeble condition. One day a young king came to visit Elisha. "Now Elisha had been suffering from the illness from which he died. Jehoash king of Israel went down to see him and wept over him. 'My father! My father!' he cried. 'The chariots and horsemen of Israel!' " (2 Kings 13:14).

Jehoash used the exact same words that Elisha used when Elijah was carried away in the chariot. "My father! My father! The chariots and horsemen of Israel!" proclaimed Elisha, standing in the smoke near the Jordan River as he rent his own clothes and took up his new mantle. Jehoash recognized that Elisha was a spiritual father and the spiritual leader of Israel. Understanding this principle of spiritual parenthood is important for any spiritual son or daughter. Spiritual fathers and mothers should be respected for their work and valued for God's kingdom. At the sound of Jehoash's salutation, Elisha rallied from his bed and rose to address the young king. Maybe this was the person God had in mind for the mantle.

Elisha devised a test to see if Jehoash might qualify to be a spiritual son. He told the king to take a bow and arrow in his hands. They opened the window, and Elisha put his hands over the king's hands, helping the king shoot the arrow in the correct direction. The king followed his directions completely; he could receive instruction, he was teachable.

Elisha's heart must have been leaping within him. He might have been thinking that he had finally found the person who could wear the mantle of prophetic power worn only by Elijah and himself. Maybe it would be Elijah, Elisha and Jehoash! Elisha tested things further. He instructed the king to take arrows and smite them on the ground. Jehoash took the arrows in his hands and smote the ground with them three times—and stopped. Elisha was angry and frustrated because of Jehoash's halfheartedness. Jehoash failed to show spiritual savvy. His attempt was lackadaisical. He should have smitten the ground aggressively in his desire for multiple victories over the Syrians. His audition was over.

Jehoash had, Elisha discovered, the outward signs of sonship but not the inward qualities. He knew the vocabulary of spiritual sonship, but though his words were correct, his heart was not right. He was not passionate. He was not intent on aggressively pursuing God's will with all he had. Jehoash could not carry the mantle. A successor was not found, so Elisha took this powerful mantle with him to his grave.

Elisha stayed with his spiritual father through the good times and the bad. He finished well. Elisha received the mantle of double portion, but his potential successors did not finish well. Gehazi was greedy, Jehu was sinful and Jehoash was halfhearted. The mantle of prophetic power for Israel fell to the ground. A prophetic discontinuation and spiritual disconnect took place for want of a true spiritual son.

We need spiritual sons and daughters whose hearts are passionately pursuing Jesus in the twenty-first century. We need people who will not use ministry for personal gain and who will finish what they start. John Mark did not finish. Timothy stayed with Paul through thick and thin. John Mark was Paul's ministry acquaintance, but Timothy was his spiritual son.

We cannot afford to have a discontinuation or disconnect in God's work. The hour is too late in God's prophetic plan for us to drop the mantle. Today's darkness must be challenged. The mantle of spiritual authority in our generation awaits those who pursue God with their whole hearts. Committed spiritual sons and daughters who demonstrate spiritual savvy are needed now!

7

Fathers (Parents) Cry, Too!

*The king was shaken. He went up to the room
over the gateway and wept. As he went, he said:
"O my son Absalom! My son, my son Absalom!
If only I had died instead of you—O Absalom,
my son, my son!"*

2 Samuel 18:33

The wail within me was strangely familiar, yet I had not experienced it for many years. My young adult son was struggling spiritually, and I was crying. A mixture of remorse, helplessness, mourning and anger at spiritual darkness was flowing through my heart. I had cried for my earthly father and cried for my spiritual father; this cry was different and familiar at the same time. It was a cry for my son, and it rose from somewhere deep inside me as I stood in the middle of the floor lamenting his name. I know my wife and daughter thought I was losing it, but they did not understand my struggle. Nor did they comprehend how deeply a father's heart can be touched. Ultimately my son Ashley would be renewed in a marvelous way, for which I am eternally grateful and proud, but in that moment, my grief was overwhelming.

David's emotions also besieged him at the news of his son Absalom's death. Mourning overtook reason as the sorrow of loss overcame the joy of victory. His cry ascended for all to hear. Though David's army won the battle, he had lost the war for his son's heart. David's grief surprised his officers. After all, Absalom had rebelled against authority, leading a revolt against his father, the king. Should David not be glad at the death of his enemy? Did Absalom not get what was coming to him? Was this not an example of divine justice at work? Why the tears? Why the sorrow-filled cry? The answer was simple—David had a parent's heart.

The account of Absalom comprises several chapters in the book of 2 Samuel. Absalom was David's son by Maacah. Absalom's full sister, Tamar, was raped by his half brother Amnon, then cast out of Amnon's house in shame (2 Samuel 13:6–18). Two years later Absalom took justice into his own hands and enforced capital punishment on Amnon his older brother (2 Samuel 13:28–29). David grieved the loss of Amnon, while Absalom fled to be with Talmai, king of Geshur (2 Samuel 13:37). Actually, Absalom did what many young men and women do when having conflict with their parents: He ran to his grandfather. Talmai was the father of Maacah, and, of course, he welcomed his grandson to the palace in Geshur.

Mind the Gap

Three years passed and David longed to reconnect with Absalom (2 Samuel 13:39). Joab, the general of David's army, persuaded David to bring Absalom back to Jerusalem, though David refused to speak to his son, nor would he allow Absalom to see his face for two more years (2 Samuel 14:28). This five-year exile from his father's presence and approval became fertile soil for a root of bitterness to grow in Absalom's heart. After all, David was the one who sent Tamar to Amnon's bedside to care for him in the first place. David failed to mete out justice on Amnon for his act of rape and rejection. David had asked Absalom to return from his grandfather's palace, and now David would not even speak to him. The distance between David and Absalom had grown, and it gave darkness and curse a place to dwell.

For more than five years, Absalom's "father wound" festered into a boiling desire for acceptance, respect and ultimately revenge. Though Absalom was by this time the oldest son and in line for David's throne, the urge to rebel within him could not be tamed, nor was the voice of patience heard. Self-control was choked out by the fast-growing roots of resentment. Absalom's descent into destruction began with feelings of betrayal and great distance from his father. His road to rebellion was paved with the building blocks of bitterness. The devil did his work in the distance between Absalom and David.

Still, the question remained: Why this deep cry from David's heart?

For those of us who are spiritual or physical parents, the answer to this question may be quite painful. David was obviously crying for Absalom, but he was also crying for himself.

Many times we forget that parents are people, too, and spiritual fathers and mothers have emotions, feelings and faults. Spiritual leadership is sometimes viewed in a surreal light. Leaders are people, yes; but we act as though they should be impervious to insult, injury and innuendo. This idealized model of leaders who are made of spiritual Teflon is simply not true. Spiritual parents are merely people. If they were not, we could never relate.

Parents are to provide a covering or protection for their children, and spiritual parents provide spiritual covering for those they are leading. This is not merely a physical protection but also a spiritual shield that guards those under its influence. When the shield is broken, those who were protected are made vulnerable to the forces of darkness.

Every time I visit London and ride the Underground, I am amused by the continual announcements made for the safety of the passengers. By far the most prevalent message is, "Mind the gap." The automated voice is reminding you of the space between the train car and the platform. This gap is where the danger lies. The same is true in our relationships with our spiritual families. Wherever relational space exists, spiritual danger is present. We must constantly be aware to "mind the gap." Additionally we should close the gap between our hearts and God. When we sin against God, we create a gap where danger resides.

David's sin of adultery with Bathsheba and murder of Uriah opened his house to the powers of destruction. When the prophet Nathan confronted David regarding his failure, the word from the Lord was stern and pointed:

> " 'Now, therefore, the sword will never depart from your house, because you despised me and took the wife of Uriah the Hittite to be your own.' This is what the LORD says: 'Out of your own household I am going to bring calamity on you. Before your very eyes I will take your wives and give them to one who is close to you, and he will sleep with your wives in broad daylight. You did it in secret, but I will do this thing

in broad daylight before all Israel.' " Then David said to Nathan, "I have sinned against the LORD." Nathan replied, "The LORD has taken away your sin. You are not going to die. But because by doing this you have shown utter contempt for the LORD, the son born to you will die."

2 Samuel 12:10–14

David's sin would carry consequences for his house. Those under his covering became vulnerable to destruction and death because of his failure. Absalom was used to carry out a portion of God's sentence against David's house, as Nathan predicted. When Absalom's rebellion was at its peak, he assumed temporary control of the throne in Jerusalem, while David fled to the eastern side of the Jordan River. Absalom took the ten women who were left behind to care for David's house and slept with them on top of the roof in front of all of Israel (2 Samuel 16:22). This was an exact fulfillment of Nathan's word to David.

God promises that He "does not leave the guilty unpunished; he punishes the children and their children for the sin of the parents to the third and fourth generation" (Exodus 34:7). How can this be? Are children responsible for their parents' sin? Are parents responsible for their children's sin? The answer to both of these questions is no. Every person has free choice, and we can choose to sin or choose to respond to God's grace and live righteously.

When a family has been damaged because of a parent's failure, however, the results can still be felt several generations later. At times this punishment of familial sin may come simply in the shame a family bears. At other times it may be visited upon them in recurring addiction or a propensity toward a particular type of failure among family members. Statisticians have noted a child of divorce has a higher likelihood to be divorced. Children of alcoholics have a higher incidence of alcoholism, and the child of an abuser is at an escalated risk for becoming an abuser.

When the news of Absalom's death reached David's ears, his heart broke within him from both sorrow and guilt. The prophet's words remained with David: The sword would not leave his house. Calamity would come from within. Death would occur.

Though I have never preached on it, I have noted in my many years of ministry a horrifying pattern that I sometimes call the *David Death Disorder*. My insights on this matter are not pleasant, nor are they something I enjoy sharing. Even as I prepare to write about it, I am concerned that what I share will add insult to injury for some or bring a sense of guilt beyond God's convicting grace. Yet for those who have not fallen, I believe this insight might prove a blessing in the long run. So, here goes.

What I call the David Death Disorder comes from my observation, through my years of ministry, of several dozen children and young teens that have died tragically. These deaths have broken the hearts of family and friends alike. They seemed out of season and a violation of the normal flow of life. Because of my role as minister and counselor for many families, I have found the following to be true: Amazingly, in every instance in which these premature deaths have occurred, one of the parents of the deceased child had committed either adultery or significant sexual sin in the past.

Now, before you jump to too many conclusions, I am sure this is not always the case. Many wonderful and godly people also lose children at an early age. History is full of accounts of missionary couples and pure-hearted servants of God losing a child. Likewise, numerous parents who fail God miserably never lose a child or suffer this kind of loss. Yet, in David's case, the loss of Bathsheba's first child was in direct relation to David and Bathsheba's sin. David's failure broke the shield of protection, and death was the result.

Absalom's death was also directly related to David's failure as a father, through his sexual sin but perhaps more through his failure to discipline, communicate love and extend forgiveness. In my opinion, this is one of the reasons for David's despairing cry. David was crying not only for Absalom; he was also crying for himself.

On the day that I stood in our home crying out for my son, much more was transpiring than met the eye. The truth is that my son was struggling in a way very similar to one of the ways I struggled as a teenager. Throughout his young life I had worked diligently to protect him from the heartache I had incurred because of my failures. I had taught, lectured, prayed and communicated my cautions often. Nevertheless he had fallen at the moment of crisis in a similar way. As I cried for him and the pain he would endure because of his sin, I was also crying in remorse for my own failure during the years of my youth.

A remorseful dirge rising from today's Church involves both spiritual parent and child. A generation of young men and women feel the vulnerability that attends a lack of spiritual covering. The widespread failure of once-trusted leaders has left a deep psychological wound on this generation of spiritual sons and daughters. Cynicism has replaced trust and spiritual paranoia has replaced peace. Many young people would prefer to just keep their distance from those in authority, including their parents. Fathers and mothers also feel the vulnerability of this day, and their anguish for their spiritual sons or daughters never seems far away. The cyclical curse of generational sin knocks at the door of millions of homes and churches; if allowed to enter, this curse will bring destruction and death.

Decreasing the Distance

What can be done? How can we stop the cycle of defeat? How can the visitation of generational failure be canceled? Though I am certainly not an expert (as proven by my own journey), God's Word seems to give us a clue for the way to stop the curse: Reduce the distance and close the gap. Sin opens a hole in the defense system of a family or church, leaving those inside vulnerable to the attack of the enemy. Failure also creates distance between people and between generations. Closing this distance is one of the key steps to a strong spiritual defense system.

Malachi 4 teaches us if the hearts of the fathers do not turn to the children and the hearts of the children do not turn to the fathers, the Lord will smite the earth with a curse. The implication is that generational distance and dissonance open the way for a curse. Even so, I personally believe that when our hearts turn toward one another, the hole in the wall is closed, the gap is mended and God's blessing is released. David's relational distance from Absalom gave a place for darkness to work. When older generations are relationally distanced from younger generations, this distance becomes a welcome mat for the curse, whether in a home or in a church.

I have said for many years that the devil works in the distance and he works in the details. Our enemy is always working to divide us, and when we fail to communicate, a gap forms, giving him space to work. Judah's continual sin brought God's judgment on the people and their capital city of Jerusalem. The Babylonians broke down the protecting wall around the city, allowing the enemy to come in like a flood. The people of Jerusalem were defeated and dispersed because their wall of protection was breached and broken.

A generation later, when Nehemiah returned to Jerusalem, he found the walls unrepaired and the city in disarray. The Temple was rebuilt, but the people were still vulnerable. Nehemiah understood that in order for the people of God to be safe, they must repair the wall, and God helped him motivate the people to unite for this purpose. When the enemies of Judah plotted to stop them, Nehemiah responded to their taunting by declaring, "The God of heaven will give us success. We his servants will start rebuilding, but as for you, you have no share in Jerusalem or any claim or historic right to it" (Nehemiah 2:20). Later Nehemiah brought the people together and established a strategy in which half the workers defended the effort while the other half built the wall. He encouraged the people, "Don't be afraid of them. Remember the Lord, who is great and awesome, and fight for your families, your sons and your daughters, your wives and your homes" (Nehemiah 4:14). By closing the gaps in the wall, they would save their families.

The same is true in our relationship with God and our fight against the curse of sin that has continued throughout the generations since Adam. When we are relationally distanced from God, our defenses are weakened, the wall of protection is breached and we cannot stand against the dynamic of darkness in our own hearts. When, on the other hand, we are in right relationship with God through Jesus and the distance between us is bridged, darkness is cast out by the light of His presence. The gap is closed. We must fight to close the gap for the sake of our children, both physical and spiritual.

When Peter followed Jesus at a distance, darkness overtook him and he denied knowing the Lord. Yet when the resurrected Jesus entered the room with Peter, and later when Jesus embraced Peter on the Galilean seashore, Peter was restored. One of the great works of the Holy Spirit since the day of Pentecost has been to reduce the distance between our hearts and heaven, bringing the life of Jesus and the power of God's Word to us. By doing this, the Holy Spirit breaks the curse through our intimacy with God and with one another. When we close the distance between us and between God and us, the unwanted visitors from generations past are deported to the land of darkness.

The familiar illustration of a man riding in the car with his wife seems applicable. The man was driving, and the wife was sitting across from him on the passenger side. She commented, "You know, we don't sit close together like we used to when we were dating and first married."

The husband responded by simply questioning, "Well, who moved?"

This is God's question to us. If we are distant from Him, then who moved away? Our heavenly Father has certainly not distanced Himself. In fact, He longs to be close to you today. He moves toward you to reduce the distance. An example of this is found in the parable of the Prodigal Son recorded in Luke 15. The younger of two sons took his inheritance and set off for a distant country, where he squandered all he had been given. Finally, out of despair, he decided to begin the long trip home, believing he must return all the way to where his father was in order to be restored. Luke notes, however, that "while he was still a long way off, his father saw him and was filled with compassion for him; he ran to his son, threw his arms around him and kissed him" (Luke 15:20). The father saw him a long way off, which meant he must have been looking toward the distant land in hope of his son's return.

When Adam and Eve sinned in the garden by eating of the Tree of Knowledge of Good and Evil, a relational distance was created between humanity and their Creator. Yet in that moment, Father God crossed the distance barrier, came to the garden again and called out to Adam, "Where are you?" (Genesis 3:9).

We see this same heart desire of God to reduce the distance when Jesus cried, "Jerusalem, Jerusalem, you who kill the prophets and stone those sent to you, how often I have longed to gather your children together, as a hen gathers her chicks under her wings, and you were not willing" (Luke 13:34). Jesus longed to bring His people close to Him like a hen gathers her chicks before a storm. He wanted to reduce the distance and thus break the curse, but Jerusalem refused to close the gap.

How about us? Are we willing to reduce relational distance in our churches and in our families? Are we willing to run to meet the wayward, to keep praying for the fallen and to continue extending our arms of love to the rebellious? Instead of regarding David's cry for his lost son Absalom as merely descriptive of what happens when sin and destruction enter a home, could we not use it as prescriptive? Death can be avoided through righteousness, love and a turning of our hearts toward one another. By God's love we can close the gap.

8

Releasing the Spirit
of Adoption

*The Spirit you received does not make you slaves,
so that you live in fear again; rather, the Spirit you
received brought about your adoption to sonship.
And by him we cry, "Abba, Father."*

Romans 8:15

hat does this mean for my local church?" This
question was asked by the pastor of one of the
fastest-growing churches in America. I had just
finished a presentation on our Empowered21 discoveries,
explaining the cry for spiritual fathers and mothers we were
hearing around the world. Considering the crescendo of
young voices attesting to this need, the pastor's question
was relevant and appropriate. *So, what?* What difference
should this make in how I do church? My answer was
simple: "I don't know what all this means for the local
church, but if churches find the answer for how to respond

to this cry, this generation will bust down the doors of those churches to get involved."

Christian denominations and local churches around the world are now discussing possible ways that this cry for spiritual parents can be met. A staff pastor from one of Asia's largest churches stated, "We are moving from a corporate culture in our church to a family culture." Another pastor shared that they are pursuing a three-generational ministry by not merely focusing on raising up spiritual sons and daughters but by raising up the next generation of spiritual fathers and mothers. Assigned mentors are used in some congregations for young people, while intergenerational efforts are being made by others to reunite parents and children in meaningful ministry.

New youth outreach models are also in experimental stages within a wide range of groups. Denominations have implemented Next Gen strategy sessions and hosted Next Gen conferences. Some have even mandated that younger men and women be given more significant leadership roles than in the past. One ministry has developed resources explaining how a church can become a totally Next Gen church by revamping their approach to everything from worship to preaching. Even parachurch ministries are creating outlets to draw in new generations, with the hope of multiplying spiritual parenting relationships. Yet the question still lingers: What more can local churches do to help answer this cry? How can ministries bring the generations together in response to the prophetic mandate of Malachi 4?

Generations Weekend

In answer to this question, the Empowered21 leadership team decided to provide resources for local churches in the form of at least one model that could be duplicated globally. We wanted something simple that could be replicated worldwide in congregations of various sizes. We intentionally sought a test church that was equipped to develop a strategic intergenerational event to provide for the possibility of spiritual parenting connections. Grace North Church in Anthem, Arizona, agreed to be our testing ground for a weekend experience that would bring multiple generations together to look at the spiritual parenting issue in a fun environment. The church hosted what was called a Generations Weekend designed to combine learning, worship, fellowship, impartation and fun. In addition they devised ways to provide a platform that would help the generations connect in fresh ways, with the hope that spiritual parent-child relationships would form. Grace North is a medium-sized, relatively young congregation with a good mix of all generations. Senior pastors Scott and Lydia Ingegneri, along with their executive pastoral team, Joe Ingegneri, Marion Ingegneri, John Mitchell and Stevie Mitchell, have a creative staff who orchestrated an amazing weekend.

The Generations Weekend focused on three distinct generations: the grandparent generation, the parent generation and the youth generation. Through intentional programming these three groups were brought together. We had intergenerational worship, intergenerational discussions, intergenerational food and intergenerational fun. Three variables were measured during the retreat: (1) increased understanding of the biblical terminology and process for intergenerational mentoring, (2) an increased sense of well-being and enrichment through increased intergenerational connections and (3) an increased desire for and intentionality toward intergenerational relationships. We also measured the response to the retreat experience itself through various survey questions.

Following the weekend, which concluded with an exclamation point of intergenerational, supernatural impartation, we discovered that in every variable, the participants had significantly moved in a positive direction. According to our findings, the overall weekend was a huge success in connecting the generations. One of the greatest discoveries we made through the Generations Weekend was that when churches make a concerted effort to bring the generations together, they obtain favor and blessing.[1]

Congregations such as Grace North Church who are willing to go the extra mile to help turn the hearts of fathers and mothers toward sons and daughters will discover a new dynamic in their churches. Synergy, trust, unity and favor will all increase because generational unity is God's will, especially in these final days before Christ returns. My prayer is that your local church makes this need a priority and realizes today's youth are desperate for your love. If they cannot find the answer to this cry within the Church, where can they turn? How do we move our congregations in this direction?

I believe one answer is that we need a fresh release of the Spirit of adoption among us. Paul tells the Romans, "For ye have not received the spirit of bondage again to fear; but ye have received the *Spirit of adoption*, whereby we cry, Abba, Father" (Romans 8:15, KJV, emphasis added). Other versions call this the Spirit of sonship. We are made sons and daughters of God both by spiritual adoption and through the new birth. "For he chose us in him before the creation of the world to be holy and blameless in his sight. In love he predestined us *for adoption to sonship through Jesus Christ*, in accordance with his pleasure and will" (Ephesians 1:4–5, emphasis added).

The Holy Spirit is the Spirit of adoption, and He works to bring us into right relationship with our heavenly Father. When the Holy Spirit is free to work in a congregation, the Spirit of adoption will be evident. God's love flowing from us will naturally move us to embrace the broken and respond to the father cry of this generation. The Church, though not the same as the nuclear, biological family, forms a new spiritual family in which we call each other brother and sister, and we recognize spiritual fathers and mothers among us. Yet this terminology can be problematic for some.

Father or Not?

A word of caution and balance seems appropriate as we talk about becoming spiritual fathers and mothers for new generations. In Matthew's gospel narrative, Jesus stated, "And do not call anyone on earth 'father,' for you have one Father, and he is in heaven" (Matthew 23:9). Later the apostle Paul wrote, "Even if you had ten thousand guardians in Christ, you do not have many fathers, for in Christ Jesus I became your father through the gospel" (1 Corinthians 4:15). Jesus told the Pharisees they should not call anyone "father," while Paul said to the Corinthians that he was their father. Was Paul contradicting the teaching of Jesus?

Observing other "spiritual father" terminology in the Bible might help our understanding of this apparent contradiction. Peter, for example, called Mark his son in 1 Peter 5:13. John called the Church "my little children" in 1 John 2:1. Stephen used the term *fathers* to address elders in Acts 7:2, and Paul used the same term to address elders in Acts 22:1. John wrote to the "little children," the "young men" and the "fathers" in 1 John 2:12–14.

Numerous times Paul spoke of being a spiritual father, and in other passages, he called Timothy, Titus and Onesimus his children in the faith. Paul exhorted Timothy that he should not rebuke an elder but should entreat him as a father (1 Timothy 5:1). Other passages that demonstrate Paul's understanding of this father principle include but are not limited to 1 Corinthians 4:17; 2 Corinthians 12:14; Philippians 2:22; 1 Thessalonians 2:11; 1 Timothy 1:2, 18; 2 Timothy 1:2–3; Titus 1:4 and Philemon 10. Even Jesus used the term *Father Abraham* in His parable of Lazarus and the rich man, recorded in Luke 16:19–31.

What are we to deduce from this contrast between Jesus' discourse to the Pharisees and the concepts of spiritual fatherhood and motherhood that appear throughout Scripture? I personally believe the best explanation revolves around emphasis and position. In Matthew 23 Jesus was speaking to the Pharisees, who loved to make a show of their outward religion. Their emphasis was distorted. They wanted to look and be perceived as more religious than anyone else. They wore their religion on their sleeves, so to speak, and they wanted everyone to know how pious they were. They worked hard on outward appearances while their hearts remained far from God. Jesus called them white tombs that had been painted on the outside but still contained dead men's bones on the inside.

The Pharisees called their teachers fathers, and they loved this title. Each was anxious to be called a father himself, even when the tangible fruit of spiritual fatherhood was not present—whereas apostles like Paul exhibited true signs of being spiritual fathers through their care, prayerfulness and willingness to suffer for their spiritual children. The Pharisees only wanted the title.

More importantly, Jesus was reminding the Pharisees that only one true father exists, and He is God—our heavenly Father. None of us on earth qualify for this position. We are simply "underfathers" or "underparents" who shepherd, care and minister under the authority of our heavenly Father. The Pharisees, in claiming to be fathers, positioned themselves in a way that blocked people's path to the real Father. Because their hearts were not right, they led people away from true fellowship with Him. Their emphasis was on their own earthly, visible, outward fatherliness and not on God's care for us. They wanted people to have a relationship with them more than with God.

Through the years the Protestant church has criticized the Catholic church for the use of the title *Father* for pastors and elders. From my study of the New Testament, I believe this criticism of title alone is too severe. The truth is that every pastor and spiritual leader should be a spiritual father or mother. Judgment and denunciation should, however, be leveled against any leader who draws people to himself or herself and away from a personal relationship with Father God.

When a priest or one who bears the official title *Father* puts himself as the mediator between God and man in such a way that people come to him instead of personally coming to Jesus, his spiritual fatherhood is negated, and he has gone too far. When people look to man for what only God can do, we are on Matthew 23 ground, which is rebuked by Jesus.

When a pastor's ego drives him to gather disciples for himself through his charismatic personality instead of using his personal charisma to point people toward Christ, he is also on Matthew 23 ground, whether he has been called "father" or not. Only God is our true Father.

Our role is simply to be earthly examples of our heavenly Father, adopting a new generation and leading them into an intimate relationship with God through Jesus Christ.

Our goal as spiritual fathers and mothers is not to have our spiritual children following us, but to use our human connection with them to help them follow God. We want all people to know God as their Father and find what most satisfies their hunger in a personal relationship with Him.

Timothy was Paul's spiritual son, and Paul consistently turned Timothy toward His heavenly Father. Paul's first words to Timothy in his first epistle to him were "Grace, mercy and peace from God the Father and Christ Jesus our Lord" (1 Timothy 1:2). Without fail Paul directed Timothy's attention toward God and God's plan for his life. This is our role as spiritual fathers and mothers as we connect with this generation. Paul understood that Timothy needed someone with skin on who could help him negotiate his spiritual journey, and Paul served in that role until his death. At the same time Paul was careful not to be the object of Timothy's worship or the source of his strength. Paul also challenged Timothy to move into spiritual fatherhood himself: "And the things you have heard me say in the presence of many witnesses entrust to reliable people who will also be qualified to teach others" (2 Timothy 2:2). Paul adopted Timothy, became his spiritual father and taught him how to look to our heavenly Father for grace and power. We must do the same.

Releasing the Spirit of Adoption

We are in desperate need of a fresh Spirit of adoption in America. Since the legalization of abortion in 1973, more than 54 million babies have lost their lives[2] in murderous procedures that are protected by our government. In many instances those having abortions have become pregnant out of wedlock and choose to abort their babies rather than raise them without a father.

If these children were protected by law in America as they should be (and I believe one day they will be), women would give birth to a wave of babies needing to be adopted. Are we ready for this? With approximately 1.2 million abortions occurring each year in America,[3] we would have a huge number of children needing people to bring them into their homes should this travesty end. The National Council for Adoption reports that in 2007 (the year the most recent statistics were available) only 18,078 of adoptions in the United States were adoptions of infants.[4] According to the Adoption History Project at the University of Oregon,

A total of approximately 125,000 children have been adopted annually in the United States in recent years. . . . Estimates suggest that adoptive families are atypical as well as few in number. Approximately 5 million Americans alive today are adoptees, 2–4 percent of all families have adopted, and 2.5 percent of all children under eighteen are adopted.[5]

Given these statistics, we would need to see a huge increase in the rate of adoption in America if abortion became illegal again. This can only happen as God softens our hearts and helps us to see with His eyes the need of the survivors.

Perhaps one way to see this release of the Spirit of adoption is to begin by spiritually adopting the hurting young people in and around our churches. Currently 1.2 billion people between the ages of 10 and 19 live on planet earth.[6] If our studies are anywhere near correct, millions of them are crying out for spiritual fathers and mothers. Without a doubt we can find dozens of these 1.2 billion youth in or around our churches. How will we respond to them? What will we do? Will we accept and exhibit a new Spirit of adoption in our day?

Losing a Father

God has brought many special friends into my life, and Wayne Hall was one of them. Wayne was a unique person. His personality was exceptional, and he had a way of knowing lots of things about lots of people. Wayne would talk to anyone, and the people he talked to were glad to tell him their stories. If you went to a restaurant with Wayne, you needed to allot extra time for Wayne's impromptu talks with anyone and everyone. His smile was infectious and his golf swing monstrous. I pastored Wayne officially for several years and unofficially for several more. Wayne also had an anointed singing voice. Whenever I wanted someone to sing a special song that I knew would bless the people, Wayne was usually my first choice as soloist. He not only sounded good; he touched your heart. Wayne, his wife, Susan, and their three girls were neighbors of ours for several years, so we became unusually close. Susan's mother and my mom were great friends, and she was the friend who helped Mom recover spiritually at the most critical time in her life.

One morning after returning from a strenuous ministry trip, Lisa and I received an emergency phone call from Susan. Wayne was being rushed to the hospital after collapsing on the floor. Could we come? We quickly dressed and met Susan at the hospital, only to discover that Wayne had suffered a brain aneurysm. For several excruciating hours, we looked on as the aneurysm filled Wayne's head with blood and ultimately took his life. It was one of the most tragic death experiences I had ever weathered. My friendship with Wayne was deep, and our love for his family made the days ahead seem overwhelming.

I was honored to preach at Wayne's funeral, which was one of the largest our community had witnessed. It was not easy, but far more difficult was looking into the eyes of his three daughters who knew that their daddy was gone. They would surely miss him for the rest of their lives. A few years after Wayne's passing, his oldest daughter, Lindsey, wrote a letter to her dad in heaven and posted it on Facebook. Lindsey gave me permission to share her letter, which I am doing so that we might gain some insight into how it feels to lose a father. I suspect that Lindsey's feelings for her natural father are also how this generation feels at times with the absence of spiritual fathers.

Dear Daddy,

It's hard to believe that four years and four months ago today, I had no clue that my life was about to change drastically. Little did I know that the next morning I would wake up to see you on the floor and call an ambulance. Little did I know I would soon lose you and never get to say good-bye. It seems like so long ago because I have gone through many stages of life, but in the realm of losing you, it seems like yesterday.

I miss your smile—the one that could light up a room. Things are changing now, and oh how I long to see you again, and have you hold me in your arms. I know I will see you again someday, and it may feel like five minutes to you, but it will be a lifetime for me. I know you are rejoicing up in heaven, and I feel you looking over me, guarding me and smiling down on my accomplishments. I hope I make you proud.

Most days I am okay and can make it through, but today is different. I just broke down. I saw a picture of you and me singing together, and I could barely breathe. This moment stopped and tugged at my heart. I can't always be strong, even though you showed nothing but strength to me. You were strong for me, Mom and the girls. I am so honored to have you as my father, and to look around and see that the impact your life has made on others and this community is irreplaceable. Your influence on me is just as great now as it was when you were alive. It's still hard for me to understand what God's purpose was for you to enter into eternity so early and leave us on earth. Of course, none of us are supposed to understand. Sometimes I get sad, angry at God or just unsure of how this happened, but my faith in Christ brings it all back together.

One thing I am thankful for is that each of us here knows that you were truly an embodiment of a man of God. You're the best, Dad. I have gone through a lot this past month, and when no one seemed to be there, I called out to God and you in heaven. I know you heard me, but it's just not the same as me being able to talk to you face-to-face in short car rides to school or around the dinner table. Your light shined so bright, Daddy. In your kind words spoken and your hugs that were famous, those things left us without a doubt concerning the love of Jesus that you had in you and I can only hope to emulate.

As you probably know, Grandpa Hall is coming home soon, too. It is comforting to know that you will be at the gate to welcome him. I hope to sing at his funeral. I am not sure I'll make it through, but I'll try my hardest. I wish I could have done this for the service to celebrate your life, but I am certain I couldn't have gotten through. Knowing that you will be there to greet Grandpa is reassuring. Even more reassuring is the fact that one day you will be greeting me with open arms. I can't wait to see you again! You never gave up on me, and for that I will be forever grateful. Even in times like this when I want to close up and become invisible, you would push me and make me want to be a better person. Also, thank you for teaching me to serve. I am learning that is one of the best things I can do for mankind. Love and serve them. And you did just that.

I am sure there are many people in Cleveland, Tennessee, that have fond memories of you. Many business leaders across the town and other cities can recall a small but powerful thing you did for them, which left your mark forever. William Lamb made my day a few days ago by telling me that he saw you in me. You always made an effort to listen to people and show them you genuinely cared. You make my heart smile. I could not be prouder to be your little girl. Several tears later, I just wanted to share that I love and miss you.

—Your Lindsey Brooke

As I am writing this chapter, Lindsey is scheduled to be married next month. Her journey has not been easy, and the pain of losing her father has been poignant, but God's people and her Christian family have made a difference. A family friend has made room for Lindsey to minister, and she sings just like her dad. One of my spiritual sons spiritually adopted Lindsey. In fact, next month when Lindsey walks down the aisle, William will participate in the ceremony and bless Lindsey as his spiritual daughter. The Spirit of adoption has made a difference.

We Can Change History

Children who are adopted are special. I have an adopted nephew named Landy, and he is as much a part of our family (perhaps even more so) as I am. Adopted children are wanted. They are not accidents, for their adoptive parents have brought them into their homes intentionally, and at great physical cost, to become their guardians. If you are adopted, you should be proud and grateful that God touched someone's heart to love you enough to become your mom and dad.

God has adopted us into His family. We are special. We are wanted, and He guards us as His own. When a church exhibits the heart of God, the Spirit of adoption will be prevalent. People can sense when they enter a sanctuary filled with love, and they can also sense whether or not a church is willing to accept them in a rejected state. When we go out of our way and bear whatever the cost to include the broken and spiritually orphaned, we are demonstrating the Spirit of adoption this generation craves.

If we are willing to extend our reach to young people in this generation, we will be positioned to change history. If we do not embrace and spiritually adopt them, history will be made anyway, but with negative effects.

One heartrending story I have often shared is about a young teenager who lived in New York City during the early 1950s. His father died before he was born, and his mother was very unstable. After moving from Louisiana to New York City, the young man's behavior grew more problematic. He was truant from school for several weeks and began acting out his violent tendencies with his mom in their home. The thirteen-year-old son was brought to accountability by the City of New York and was assigned to a probation officer named John Carro.

In the process of evaluating the young man, authorities discovered that he had some psychological problems. When the courts and city tried to involve the boy's mother in an appropriate treatment process, she fled the state, abandoning her thirteen-year-old son and leaving him in the custody of the juvenile delinquency courts. Officer Carro, knowing this young man needed help, decided to see if he could find an agency that would take the young man and give him the treatment as well as the home and love he needed. Officer Carro would testify a decade later that agencies across New York City refused the young man. He could not find anyone that would reach out and "adopt" this troubled boy during his critical early teen years.

A majority of youth assistance agencies were governed by churches in those days, yet every church agency Mr. Carro petitioned turned the boy away. Most of the rejections were because the young man came from a Lutheran background, and the particular agency would not accept someone from that denomination. Catholic, Jewish and multiple Protestant groups all said no. He was not welcome. Can you imagine that a needy young man would be refused help because of his religious background?

Has your church ever turned a young life away because they were not like the people in that church? Have you ever rejected God's spiritual adoption process for helping someone from another generation because it was not convenient or easy? Churches across New York City in the early 1960s did, leaving the young teenager even more rejected. Abandoned by family and rejected by the Church, the course of this young man's life continued toward destruction. The Spirit of adoption in the churches of New York City might have changed history: The young man's name was Lee Harvey Oswald![7]

9

When Your Pain
Becomes Your Platform

*And we know that in all things God works for
the good of those who love him, who have been
called according to his purpose.*

Romans 8:28

Brilliant sunshine flooded the Bogotá, Colombia, park
as we made our way to the afternoon rally. The people
gathered from across the city to form a crowd of
approximately 100,000 on that brilliant Latin American
afternoon. The huge crowd had been brought together
by a ministry called G12 for an evangelistic outreach.
Standing and sitting on the ground, the mass of humanity spread across the park field for a significant distance.
Some had banners exalting Jesus, and others wore identical
T-shirts to identify their church groups. Children, babies,

grandparents and teenagers all blended together, bubbling with a sense of excitement about the day.

I was scheduled to speak at the rally and invite people to Christ. Since I only had a few moments to speak, I had prayed sincerely about what message I would deliver. American president Woodrow Wilson was once asked how long it would take him to prepare for a speech. He answered, "If you want fifteen minutes, it will take about two weeks. If you want two hours, I am ready now!" I have found that this is true for me as well. Usually, the shorter the speaking segment, the longer my prep time will be.

As I prayed and reflected, it was clear to me that my message needed to be much more testimony than theology. I decided to share my personal story and the story of my family, blended with a scriptural call to receive Jesus, the miracle worker. We experienced a wonderful moment of grace, tears and God's presence. At the end of the brief message, approximately 30,000 people stood to commit their lives to Christ. This was the largest single response to receive Jesus as Savior that I had witnessed up to that time in my ministry. As He had many times before, God turned my pain into my platform, and hurting hearts were healed.

When life is difficult and we pass through seasons of pain, we should be cognizant of the fact that if we love Him and trust Him, God is working all things for our good. We should also realize that God never wastes anything, including the pain of those who serve Him. When we are comforted amid our struggles and distress, we can share with others what we have discovered to help them also find comfort. Jesus brought healing to the world through His wounds, as Isaiah wrote: "He was pierced for our transgressions, he was crushed for our iniquities; the punishment that brought us peace was on him, and by his wounds we are healed" (Isaiah 53:5). Jesus was wounded internally and suffered internal bleeding through His bruises. He was wounded externally in His head, hands, feet, back and side. All of these areas were opened to allow His pure blood to flow out on the earth. These areas of wounding made provision for our healing—Jesus' wounds released life through the shedding of His blood.

Amazingly, His resurrection did not remove His wounds. Jesus rose from the dead on a Sunday morning in a new body that was no longer restricted to the earthly dimensions of time or space. Though He ate food in His new body, He could also walk through walls. Yet John wrote that when the Lord appeared to the disciples to show them He was fully alive, "He showed them his hands and side" (John 20:20). The following Sunday Jesus invited Thomas to touch the scars in His hands and side. Jesus was identified by His wounds, and so are we.

Overcoming the Acid Test

My father left our family when I was five years old. At that time we were living in a church supervisor's parsonage in West Virginia, a wonderful place for a little boy, with beautiful grounds, an orchard and an abundance of places to play. Some of my earliest memories are of the deep West Virginia snows, the beautiful sky, my special bedroom and the warmth of our home. My utopia was shattered the day my parents separated, though I did not understand all the ramifications at the time. We were soon asked to move out of our home in order to make room for the next state bishop. Someone else would now enjoy my orchard and my special bedroom.

Of the numerous effects of family breakups, one of the most devastating that divorced families must endure is the depletion of their financial resources. The selfishness of separation and divorce takes its toll in real dollars. The disbursement of wealth is rarely fair and is usually never enough. When my father left, my mother, Joyce, had no job and no promise of one nearby. What could we do? Mom decided to go home, back to the Owensboro, Kentucky, area where her parents lived. Their little town of Knottsville had a Catholic church, two saloons and a store as its main attractions. Mom found a job, and everyone worked to provide for this enlarged, multigenerational family.

On the move to Kentucky, I was riding in an old flatbed truck with our furniture strapped down in the truck bed. It was a fun ride for a five-year-old boy; I stood on the seat between two big, burly West Virginians, who were friends of the family. The gearshift at my feet, the rattle of the old vehicle and all the accompanying smells of a 1960s farm truck filled my senses. We would have made a wonderful *Beverly Hillbillies* commercial, except we were moving from hillbilly country in West Virginia to hillbilly country in Kentucky.

Suddenly we heard a thud. I looked out the driver's-side window and saw two wheels with an axle between them rolling down the highway. The entire back end of the truck fell out. My burly driver friend tried to guide the truck to the shoulder—at least what shoulder existed on old Highway 60 in eastern Kentucky—but we hit a hole in the pavement. Our vehicle, laden with our broken family's possessions, gave a heave and began rolling.

Now, standing over a gearshift in a rattletrap truck is not the best position to be in, especially during a wreck. I was tossed into the roof of the truck cab as we continued to roll. Adding to this distress was the fact that an old car battery was lying in the floorboard of the truck. When we began our upside-down excursion, the seals holding the battery acid within the container came off. Dangerous acid sloshed around the cab as if spraying from an out-of-control water hose. Much of the acid fell on my five-year-old frame, saturating my clothes. By the time the truck came to rest, all of us inside were bruised but alive. My clothes, however, were drenched in battery acid.

My grandparents and one of my sisters were traveling in a car in front of the truck. Thankfully they saw the truck flip over and quickly made an emergency U-turn. What they found when they returned to us was pitiful. Clothes were strewn across the field, and busted furniture was everywhere. The scene looked as though a mini-tornado had made a direct hit on the truck, swirling contents in every direction. They also found our two friends and me crawling out of the truck's cab.

My grandmother grabbed me to see if I was all right. Immediately Mammy realized that my clothes were drenched in battery acid, so she ripped my acidic clothing from my body. Even my undergarments were contaminated, so they had to be removed, also. Worse, any possible change of clothing was scattered across several yards of the field alongside the highway. There I stood before God, and every car traveling on Highway 60 that day, in my birthday suit. It was humiliating, embarrassing and cold. Insult had been added to the injury of my father's departure.

In many ways this generation must feel like I felt that fateful day as their physical and spiritual parents fail them. I felt vulnerable, wrecked, disoriented, humiliated and cold. Today's youth may sense a lack of covering, leaving them standing by life's roadside unclothed, while their pain is on display.

I have wondered over the years what Lucifer must have thought during those moments I stood by the highway in Kentucky. Here was a little boy whose life had been turned upside down, whose heart had been crushed. I was born with a God-ordained destiny, but it appeared that this destiny would come to a halt and be forever confined because of my father's sins. Satan must have smiled.

Yet I have also wondered what *God* must have thought that day. He saw my pain, He knew about my father's sin, He saw the battery acid and He knew the future. Because of that foreknowledge, I believe God smiled, too. The little boy covered in battery acid, standing naked before the world with his heart crushed, still had a future, and he still had a destiny. In fact, when Satan was doing his worst, God was preparing to do His best.

Perhaps as you are reading this book, your world has recently been turned upside down. A poison from darkness has drenched your soul and is eating away at your spiritual covering. You feel vulnerable. You are hurting and cold. You are broken, and in some ways you feel the entire world is watching. Maybe you started well, but the wounds you have incurred have left you helpless and powerless on the side of life's road. You feel as though Satan is smiling. If that is true, I want to assure you that God is smiling, too. He is smiling because He knows the future and sees what you could be. He still believes in you. He knows your potential. You were born with a destiny, and this moment of pain will not stop God's plan for your life, unless you allow it. Not only can you survive, but you can thrive. In fact, though Satan is doing his worst, God will use this moment to prepare you for His best.

But God!

The years following our move to Kentucky were good despite my pain. I was reared by two wonderful grandparents, and my mother did her best to provide all she could for us. Mammy and Pop built me a new bedroom, and their plot of land became a wonderful playground for a growing boy. By the time I was a teenager, however, the manifestations of my brokenness were impossible to hide. I plunged into a variety of vices, everything a teenager could do in 1970s small-town America (and that was quite a lot). The path I followed was taking me far from God. Controlled by my passions and my own selfishness, I was on a journey with a trajectory that did not look good. No gambling man would have wagered on a turnaround in my life.

But God! I have always loved those words from Scripture; they and He make all the difference. In Paul's correspondence to the Ephesians, he acknowledged that we were children of wrath as we fulfilled the desires and lusts of the flesh. "*But God*, who is rich in mercy, for his great love wherewith he loved us, even when we were dead in sins, hath quickened us together with Christ, (by grace ye are saved)" (Ephesians 2:4–5, KJV, emphasis added).

I was lost and headed toward destruction, *but God* came to my rescue and changed my life. In the summer between my junior and senior years of high school, I gave my life to Jesus Christ. Within weeks I was filled with the Holy Spirit and won my first convert to the Lord. In my final year of high school, I went from being the foulest-mouthed player on the basketball team to the one they asked to pray before ball games. My encounter with Jesus transformed me from the inebriated young man they had to carry out of school functions to the person chosen to pray at his graduation ceremony. *But God* made the difference.

Between the pain of being abandoned by my earthly father and the joy of personally connecting with my heavenly Father, things also began to change for my dad. After walking out the door of the West Virginia parsonage for the last time, he spent the next several years wandering on the borders of a spiritual wasteland. Divorce is destructive. Dad tried to preach some during this time, but it was not the same. He also married again and remained with his new wife for several years. It appeared that this would be his lot, until one day God spoke clearly to him while he was mowing the lawn. According to his own testimony, he heard God's voice say that he must leave this situation, and that this was his last chance. In obedience to God, Dad divorced his second wife and began to pursue his ministry again from a place of brokenness and humility.

By the time I accepted Christ as Savior, Dad was preaching in various churches across the country. My first ministry trip with him took place during the same summer of my conversion. It was strange and yet a blessing. The trip took us from Kentucky to Arizona, on to Montana and back, and during those weeks we experienced the small beginnings of a father-son relationship that would flourish later in life.

One of my great memories from that trip is of a three-person prayer meeting in Rockford, Illinois. Dad and I walked with Pastor Keith, one of Dad's friends, to the church one afternoon to pray together. During the prayer Pastor Keith laid his hands on my head and spoke prophetically that I would take the Gospel of Jesus Christ to the nations of the world. This was a bit heavy for a sixteen-year-old who was on his first trip west of the Mississippi River and had never been on an airplane. Dad and I would laugh about this moment later. We always respected Pastor Keith for his spiritual obedience, especially now that I have

135

preached in person in more than eighty different nations and our television program is presently seen in more than one hundred and fifty nations every week. Only God could have gotten me through my roadside "acid" test and into fulfilling my prophetic purpose.

Reconciled by Love

Following high school I attended Western Kentucky University with my high school sweetheart, Lisa. She and I were married before our last year of college. During this time my relationship with my natural father continued to improve, and the impact of spiritual fathers (and mothers) on my life became very significant. Pastors, bishops and godly men and women in our church all helped form me for Christ during those first years following my conversion. The value of intergenerational relationships should never be underestimated.

As I write this chapter, I am still impacted by those whose purity, faithfulness and love for me profoundly shaped my life, helping me become all I am today. Spiritual fathers and mothers believed in me and spoke into my life day after day and week after week. The pastor of our home church, the pastor of the church we attended during college, the church overseer in our state, my Sunday school teachers and even an aged prayer warrior (who spiritually adopted me) each made a significant difference just because they cared. I am not sure how conscious they were of their effect on my life, but the influence of their love has been profound. The spiritual parenting journey is not difficult; it is simple. Love works. When a godly adult takes time to show, in a practical way, how much God cares about a young person, it makes a huge eternal difference.

In the years following my conversion, my father continued pursuing his ministry and serving the Lord. My mom, however, was still far from the mark spiritually. Her bitterness overtook her heart, and the results were disastrous. Mom also was married again for a short time following my parents' divorce, and she also divorced her second husband. Statistics on divorce are much worse for the second marriage than they are for a first marriage. This is because people carry their baggage with them into the second marriage. In many instances the pain-filled emotional suitcases they carry are just too heavy for the new marriage to haul through life. Mom tried everything to find satisfaction and peace, but nothing worked. It never does when you are out of God's will.

I prayed for my mother many, many times, and I carried an almost inescapable burden for her until one night at the altar. At an evening service I was interceding and crying out verbally for Mom's salvation. During my moments of prayer, I seemed to be carried away in a vision and saw her riding on a white horse. I believe I heard God's voice say, "She will be all right." I told my sister Donna what I had seen and shared my belief that everything was going to be all right. I believed Mom and Dad were going to be reunited, with Mom leading the way. Following that evening service my burden for Mom shifted from despair to expectancy. Years later I learned that Donna shared my vision with Mom, and these words haunted her in her alone moments. God used them to draw her back to Him.

Shortly after Lisa and I were married, my mother awoke one Sunday morning and heard the Holy Spirit whisper that it was her day. Simultaneously Donna, who was at church, was impressed to go home. When she arrived, she found Mom in tears. Quickly they called one of Mom's best friends, who met them at the church and prayed with my mother until her burden of failure and guilt were lifted. Mom rose from that moment of repentance and forgiveness to begin a miraculous journey. She asked Donna to travel to Florida with her. When Donna asked why she wanted to go to Florida, Mom replied, "I want to find your dad. I need to ask his forgiveness."

So Mom and Donna made the nearly twelve-hour trek to Brooksville, Florida, where Dad was planting a small church. They arrived at the very small, modest trailer where Dad was living and knocked on the door. When my father answered the door, he said, "Joyce, I have been expecting you." No one had told him she was coming to Florida.

Over the next few days, miracles occurred. Fifteen years of separation and divorce had created relational walls that seemed insurmountable. With both of them now reconciled to Christ, perhaps reconciliation to one another was possible. They talked and thought about their next steps. What did this mean? What should they do? It was not an easy journey. At one point Dad told Mom very bluntly, "I don't think I love you anymore." At that critical moment Mom replied, "That's okay, because I have enough love for both of us." What an amazing, courageous statement to offer a man who had abandoned her fifteen years earlier.

My mother and father, both of whom had previously strayed far away from God and seemed destined for darkness, were reunited with Christ and with one another. A wonderful family friend performed their second marriage ceremony. Mom moved into the little trailer in Brooksville, Florida, to join Dad in his church plant. Soon they began evangelizing and pastoring in a variety of locations. For the next 32 years, my parents shared life and ministry together, until Dad went home to be with the Lord. Their love for one another grew exponentially during the second phase of their marriage, and all of us were proud of Mom for having enough love for both of them in order to get started again. It is simple. Love works.

The Power of Your Pain

Little did we know when I stood on the side of Highway 60 naked and covered in battery acid that someday I would stand before thousands of people around the world to declare the good news of Jesus Christ. My early ministry years were focused on young people. During a time in our society fraught with rapidly escalating divorce and family deterioration, I was able to share hope with young men and women whose hearts were breaking because of their parents' failures. This is what happened in Bogotá, Columbia, and it has happened at least a thousand times through the years of my ministry.

One of the reasons God was smiling that day on Highway 60 is because He knew that the pain and shame I was enduring was preparing me for exactly the task He was designing for me. Perhaps God even smiled because He knew that someday I would write this book, challenging all of us to find our healing in Him and become spiritual parents for new generations.

Hurting people will identify with someone who has known pain, especially when the person has found healing and grace for that pain. Like Jesus, our wounds become a place of ministry, and when we allow others to touch our scars, hope revives in their hearts. As we surrender completely to Christ, He uses everything in our lives—the good, the bad and the ugly—to redeem us for His glory. God can even take our worst mistakes and turn things around, using the moments of our greatest shame for His greatest good.

God does not cause all of our pain, but He will use it. God did not make my father leave our home. He did not make the truck turn over on the highway, and He did not make me act out my lusts and hunger for love in unholy ways as a teenager. What He did was redeem me completely to use everything in my life—even my messes. I witnessed the power of this redemption to touch the lives of other people through a special *World Impact* television program in which I interviewed Mom and Dad about their story. Their journey has blessed millions of people around the world, and this episode of *World Impact* has received the greatest response of any television program we have ever aired.

How about you? What wounds are you carrying? What is your story? If you are a young person whose life has been turned upside down, exposing your heart and making you vulnerable, please know God is smiling because He sees the potential that remains in you. If you are a father or mother who has "blown it" with your children, you must understand it is not too late. The God who made the sun stand still can give you the moments needed to ask for forgiveness and make things right. If you are a church leader whose failure has hurt a few or injured a thousand, then stop. Generations will be affected by your decisions.

Give your mess to the Lord. Even Samson's failure with Delilah became a gateway to great victory for God's people, for more Philistines were annihilated during Samson's death than were destroyed throughout his life. Finally, if you are a young person whose heart has been broken by your spiritual father or mother, remember that God will use even this for His glory. Allow Him to cleanse your wounds, transforming them into a scar that will bless those around you.

You may never preach in front of large crowds or share with millions through television. You may not travel to a multitude of nations, but God has positioned you to make a difference for someone. Your scars come from your story, and your story is what people want to hear. A young person needs you to care. Do not make it complicated, just share God's love and share your life. Your pain has given you a platform.

10

A Father's Love

This is love: not that we loved God, but that he loved us and sent his Son as an atoning sacrifice for our sins.

1 John 4:10

For I am convinced that neither death nor life, neither angels nor demons, neither the present nor the future, nor any powers, neither height nor depth, nor anything else in all creation, will be able to separate us from the love of God that is in Christ Jesus our Lord.

Romans 8:38–39

We had just settled in for the evening when the phone rang. At various times in my life, a telephone call has brought joy, triumph, elation and good news. I have learned of babies being born, engagements being made and resources being shared. The ability for information to travel through the phone or over the

Internet has been a great source of immediate joy. Thank God for technology.

Of course I have experienced other kinds of phone calls. I have received calls from crying mothers asking me to pray for their children, calls from angry parishioners that turned my stomach, calls informing me of emergencies that drove me into action and even calls relating the sad news of someone's death. The call I received this particular November evening fit into the "not so welcome" category. My mother was on the other end of the line. Dad was in the hospital, and the news was not good. The doctors thought that he might only have a few hours to live.

My father had fought heart problems with all of the accompanying struggles for years. Open heart surgery, medications, modified diets, regular exams and the slow deterioration resulting from congestive heart failure were all part of his journey. Through it all Dad remained strong in spirit, preaching, traveling and ministering as much as possible. He had a special ministry to hurting preachers, who seemed to flock to him. No one was too beat up or broken down for Dad. He loved them all. Dad's pain and spiritual scars from the past gave him a special empathy for other ministers who were struggling. Most of them would tell you that no one had ever been willing to love them the way Dad loved them.

Dad was a spiritual father to many ministers, and he was passionate about it, especially in his later years. He simply would not quit. All of us were amazed at his sheer will to live and his ability to endure exhausting pain while still exhibiting a sweet, loving joy. He taught our family more in the last years of his life than at any other time by showing us how to live through physical pain in order to minister to others. Now he would show us how to die.

Miraculous Good-bye

A four-hour car trip followed the phone conversation. Lisa and I arrived at Dad's hospital room in the early morning hours. Mom, my sisters, Donna and Marqueta, and my niece Megan were waiting for us. As I slipped into the room, things were quiet. Dad lay motionless on the bed as the sound of his steady breathing filled the air. Gone was the smile of greeting I could always count on and the crazy "Hey, hey, hey!" he would exclaim. The ever-present glimmer of life in his eyes had departed. There would be no talk of church or ministry this visit. He was in the quiet place so many enter just before crossing over.

I have been with dozens of people in this quiet place that comes just before death. It is like a spiritual waiting room or terminal seating area. People seem to be suspended somewhere between where they have been and where they are going. In reality they are somewhere between this world and the next, between heaven and earth. Things seem suspended until all is ready.

Perhaps God is making sure a special spot is completely prepared for the one joining Him in heaven, or perhaps He is removing the tethers of earth slowly, one by one, before releasing that person into His presence forever. Like those quiet moments spent waiting for your name to be called at the doctor's office or waiting for the boarding announcement for a flight, this heavenly waiting room is quiet but filled with anticipation. Of course it is also a moment we dread, for none of us like to say good-bye. Dad was in this waiting room that morning, and we were not sure how long we had before saying our last earthly good-bye. Perhaps days, perhaps hours.

My father lived a full life. His was a life with some mistakes and failures, but it was also a life filled with great joy and amazing victories. Dad had an anointed ministry that touched people around the world, as did his love without condemnation. Everywhere he went, which was anywhere he was asked to preach, he made friends easily. Marqueta, Donna and I shared our father with dozens of spiritual sons and daughters whom he loved as his own.

Yet after all the miles traveled, the pulpits filled, the sermons preached, the prayers prayed and the lives touched, it was simply our family who gathered in the room with Dad to wait on God's call. Gone were the three-piece suits, the prophet's voice, the anointed energy of a man on fire for Christ and the inner strength that had fought off death before. Now it was just us, waiting with my father for God's final call in his life.

Daylight came and the waiting continued. Mom and Donna were exhausted. They had borne the brunt of Dad's hospitalization and remained with him day and night. It seemed a good time for them to take a break, so I sent them out for a shower and breakfast. Only Lisa, Marqueta, Megan and I remained with Dad. Lisa had recently been with her grandmother at her passing, and she mentioned to me how she wished she had read more Scripture and prayed more with her grandmother during her final moments. She suggested I read the Bible or pray more with Dad. Though I have been a preacher and leader for many years, I learned a long time ago that Lisa's insights and discernment were some of God's gifts to our ministry, so like a good husband I decided to read Scripture. Thank God for the Gideon Bible in the drawer beside Dad's bed.

I knelt by the bedside, as I had throughout the morning hours, and began reading Dad's favorite passages. I read his favorite psalms and some of the accounts from which he preached often, like the stories of Lazarus and the woman at the well. I even read the last two chapters of the book of Revelation, which give us insight into heaven. It seemed that the more I read the more grace I sensed in the room, and the more Scripture I wanted to read. God's Word is powerful, even in the valley of death. After I read for some time, we began to sing—first a few hymns and then a couple of praise and worship choruses. The hospital became a sanctuary as God's presence filled each of us and seemed to fill the room.

Dad had shared with me many times over the years his belief that men tend to die the way they live. If they live by the sword, they die by the sword. If they live giving love, they die receiving love, and so on. This has been evident numerous times over the last few years as some of the earth's vilest and most violent men, men like Muammar Gaddafi and Saddam Hussein, have died vile and violent deaths. Dad lived in and for the presence of God most of his life. Nothing thrilled him more than God's immediate presence in a worship service and witnessing the power of God's Word in action. Thus it seemed fitting that in the last hours of Dad's life, God's Word was being read and worship was being lifted. He was going to die the way he lived.

Ultimately our makeshift hospital-room choir began to sing two songs Dad really loved, "I Love You, Lord" and "We Exalt Thee." As we sang these inspired choruses, I found myself kneeling again by Dad's bed, holding his hand. Throughout the morning he had not acknowledged my presence, but now, as God's presence filled the room, he stirred slightly. Suddenly he opened one eye clearly and stared right at me, as if to say, "Billy, I know you are here; I love you, and all is well." Then Dad breathed his final breaths and departed from us. His appointment time, his boarding time for eternity, had arrived. Everything was ready in heaven, and the last tether of earth was broken. His waiting was over. He was finally home.

While I still knelt by my father's bed, emotions flooded over me in waves too large to comprehend. My best friend in ministry had just departed. The voice of the greatest cheerleader my life had ever known was now silent. There would be no more calls of encouragement or words of insightful wisdom. His cherished hugs of understanding would now cease, and his eyes filled with pride and approval were now closed in death. Grief swept over my soul, and sadness filled my heart. I have always hated good-byes. I especially hated this one.

At the same time, other emotions flooded my soul. My heart seemed like the Cape of Good Hope in Africa, near where the Atlantic and Indian Oceans meet. Around this unique peninsula, diverse currents and waters of varied temperature collide. The results are spectacular and dangerous, producing beautiful vistas as well as numerous shipwrecks. The waves are tumultuous and amazing. Kneeling by the bedside of my departed father was a Cape of Good Hope moment. Grief and joy collided in my heart with currents of both tears and gratitude.

God had just allowed me—despite all of my global travels and heavy schedule—to be at my father's bedside reading Scripture and singing to him as he left this world. I could have been halfway around the world, as I am while writing this chapter, but God ordered my steps to be home when Mom called. We could have been doing a thousand things at that moment, but we were worshiping, praying and reading Scripture. Dad could have passed while in surgery or in a night of sleep, but he did not. We were with him, and my heart swelled with gratitude for God's kindness to me in this.

Dad's lifetime fight with sin and Satan was over. Victory had been won. His flight home was instant, and he was already enjoying the presence of Jesus in heaven. I rejoiced in spite of my tears.

I Love, I Love, I Love You!

I decided several weeks ago to begin writing this particular chapter on the one-year anniversary of Dad's passing as a tribute to one of the greatest spiritual fathers I have ever known. As my travel schedule would orchestrate, this one-year anniversary is actually beginning (I waited to cross the international date line to begin writing) while I am somewhere over the Pacific Ocean, on my way to Australia. Though I have preached in more than eighty nations of the world, to my knowledge, this is the only nation where Dad preached and I have not. This morning, on the one-year anniversary of his death, I will minister for the first time "Down Under."

As I have written this chapter (whatever time it is), the emotions have flowed like a river despite the travel exhaustion I feel. I have laughed, and I have wept strongly. (I have been very glad that they keep the plane so dark.) Yes, I have wept with those same mixed emotions over my father's passing, and yes, I have wept with joy in remembering my father's love. At the same time I have wept for you and millions of others like you. Let me explain.

Only a couple of weeks before the morning of Dad's eternal appointment with Jesus, I was at his bedside when he began the process of telling everyone good-bye. He was not quite in the spiritual waiting room yet, but the prognosis was not good, and Dad seemed to know his time was short. In fact, he seemed like a man on a mission as he began communicating to each individual his love and concern. He was able to lay hands on William Samuel, my youngest grandchild and his youngest great-grandchild. My daughter, Sara (Samuel's mom), along with her husband, Shaun, and daughter, Abigail, were providentially on furlough from Paraguay, where they lead a home for abandoned children. Dad took special time to pray for each of his grandchildren and had unique moments with each of his children, including me. Though dying, he was more concerned about giving than receiving. He continued to minister to others in every way possible until he could speak no longer.

His moments with me during those last weeks of his life will always be some of the most treasured times I have known. This is especially true of one particular day.

As I entered Dad's hospital room, he seemed anxious and glad to see me. We shared a few pleasantries along with our normal ministry updates, and then Dad began saying he loved me. It really did not matter what I wanted to talk about over the next couple of hours; he kept saying that one thing over and over and over. He would look me right in the eye and say, "I love you, Billy." He seemed unable to say it enough, as if he was trying to drive those words into my very soul. I guess it worked, because as I reflect on those most precious of moments, tears are running down my cheeks. Oh, the treasure of having your father say he loves you!

That afternoon Dad seemed to know that this might be our last time to really communicate, and it was. The one thing he wanted me to understand and remember—beyond his pride in me, beyond our special friendship, beyond any ministry situation, beyond any practical earthly concern, beyond anything at all—was him saying, "I love you." He wanted me to remember and know that it was true.

The years of estrangement, the days of fatherlessness I endured, the moments of bitterness and misunderstanding, the shame of failure and the tears of abandonment had long ago been washed away in God's sea of grace. Yet Dad's fervency in communicating his love, despite his own pain that day in his hospital room, continues to echo in my heart even now, creating a tsunami of gratitude and praise. My father loved me. Oh, how wonderful! I will forever rest in my earthly father's love. I weep tears of joy to have this treasure, but I also weep because millions of men and women, boys and girls have never heard these words from their earthly fathers.

Maybe you are one of them. Perhaps you have never heard your father utter the words, "I love you," or perhaps they were just words, without proof of any kind. Maybe you do not know who your father is or have never even met him personally.

Even more difficult is when your father has spoken words of hate and anger. Your heart longs for affirmation, and your soul yearns for love. Somewhere deep within you are waves of grief roiling beneath the hardened surface you may portray. You of all people understand the father cry of this generation. It is a cry all of us can understand because it rises from every human heart. It is a cry for covering, a cry for hope and a cry for love. It is a cry that today's Church must hear.

After all is said and done, after all our great efforts, programs and ministry intentions are fulfilled, life really boils down to just this. Men and women, boys and girls simply need someone to be their spiritual father or mother and say, "I love you," in a way that they can know is true.

Bruce Reynolds died quietly in a small town in New York. During his funeral people learned a unique secret. Twenty-five years before his death, Bruce's first wife left

him for another man and took his only child, a girl named
Ivah. Bruce supported his daughter financially, though she
lived far away and he could not see her. Bruce resolved in
his mind to love his daughter anyway. Every week for 25
years, Bruce wrote Ivah a letter. She seldom wrote back,
but Bruce kept writing to tell her he loved her. When a
series of strokes made it impossible for Bruce to write, he
dictated the letters to his second wife, who sent them to
Ivah. Bruce communicated his love to Ivah through more
than 1,300 letters written during those 25 years because
he wanted his little girl to know he loved her.[1]

This is what the greatest Father in all of history wants
us to know more than anything else. Jesus' coming and
especially Jesus' dying was our heavenly Father saying, "I
love you." The Bible is God's love letter to us. Every day for
almost two thousand years, God has reminded us of how
He loves us: Every time you read Scripture or take Com-
munion. Every time you feel His presence or are hugged by
one of His children. Every time you sit down to eat or you
sleep well through the night. Each time you hold a baby
in your arms, see a beautiful sunset or hear the whisper of
God's voice, your heavenly Father is saying, "I love you!"
Though your earthly parents or even your spiritual parents
may have failed to communicate love, in this regard, your
heavenly Father will never fail.

After writing the first part of this chapter, I experienced
a unique moment. Lisa and I made our way to the church
in Perth, Australia, where I was to preach during the first
Sunday morning service. I was excited to be ministering
in Australia for the very first time, and Perth is a beautiful city. It has more than a million people, but it is a long
way from anywhere else. In fact, Perth is the most isolated
metropolis on the planet.

Upon arriving at the church, we had a brief meeting with Pastor Margaret Court, the great tennis star, and her husband, Barry. Following this, Lisa and I were ushered into the sanctuary, where worship was already in progress. Toward the end of the very contemporary and fresh worship session, the leader shifted to two older choruses. I learned later that someone sang those choruses in a prayer meeting a couple of weeks earlier, and they decided to revisit these old songs on this Sunday morning. Amazingly, the two choruses were "I Love You, Lord" and "We Exalt Thee." We sang these exact two choruses in the exact same order at Dad's bedside the day he died.

After spending the night writing the chapter you have just read on the one-year anniversary of Dad's passing, I visited a church that I had never attended, located in the most isolated metropolis on earth. The worship leader in that church was singing the exact two choruses in the exact same order that we sang when Dad passed, and they had not sung those songs during a worship service in years. I was spiritually overwhelmed and deeply touched. What did this mean? Why would this happen? For me the message was clear. This time it was not my earthly father saying, "Billy, I love you." It was my heavenly Father saying over and over again, "Billy, I love you, I love you, I love you, I LOVE YOU!"

The Father's arms are open wide. His love is stronger than death. He knows your pain. He sees your struggle, and He still wants you! You were born to be His child, and He delights to be your Father. When no one else responds, and the people around you seem deafened by their own selfishness, Abba Father has not turned away. Lift your voice to Him. He will respond to your *FATHER CRY!*

Notes

Introduction

1. Maureen Cleave, "How Does A Beatle Live? John Lennon Lives Like This" (March 4, 1966), The Beatles Ultimate Experience, http://www.beatlesinter views.org/db1966.0304-beatles-john-lennon-were-more-popular-than-jesus-now -maureen-cleave.html.

2. Oral Roberts to students in the Oral Roberts University Chapel Service, January 26, 1973, Oral Roberts University Archives.

3. Steve Turner, "John Lennon's Born-Again Phase" (January 3, 2007), *Christianity Today*, http://www.christianitytoday.com/ct/2007/januaryweb-only/001 -22.0.html. In this excerpt from *The Gospel According to the Beatles*, Turner shares more details about how John Lennon's brief salvation experience impacted his life and interpersonal relationships. He also relates the negative influence of his wife Yoko, which led to his ultimate rejection of Christianity and return to depression.

Chapter 2: Awakening to the Cry

1. Michael Flood, "Fatherhood and Fatherlessness," Discussion Paper 59 (Canberra, Australia: Australia Institute, 2003), 4. Flood's discussion paper looks at the growing problem of fatherlessness in Australia. He discusses the positive trend of fathers who were still with their families wanting to get more involved but then notes the negative trend of less father presence for the children of Australia, with greater divorce, abandonment, nonmarital childbearing and nonmarital cohabitation. Flood's insights would hold in most Western nations, including the United States.

2. "Single Parenting and Children's Academic Achievement" (accessed February 26, 2012), Adoption.com, http://library.adoption.com/articles/single-parenting-and-childrens-academic-achievement.html.

3. Rose M. Kreider and Jason Fields, "Living Arrangements of Children: 2001," Current Population Reports P70–104 (Washington, D.C.: U.S. Census Bureau, 2005), 3.

4. Ibid.

5. Nancy R. Gibbs, et al., "Time Archive: Where Are All the Fathers?" (June 16, 2007), *Time*, http://www.time.com/time/magazine/article/0,9171,978762,00.html.

6. Ibid.

7. "Fathering in America" (June 18, 2009), National Center for Fathering, http://www.fathers.com/documents/research/2009_Fathering_in_America_Summary.pdf.

8. "The Father Factor" (accessed March 21, 2012), National Fatherhood Initiative, http://www.fatherhood.org/media/consequences-of-father-absence-statistics. See also "Fatherhood/Male Involvement Facts" (accessed March 21, 2012), Santa Clara County Fatherhood/Male Involvement Collaborative, http://www.sccfmic.org/facts.html.

9. Dennis Hunt, "The pain behind the 'Partridge,'" *USA Today*, January 6, 2000, final edition.

10. J. H. Bray, "Children in Stepfamilies: Assessment and Treatment Issues," in *Understanding Stepfamilies: Implications for Assessment and Treatment,* ed. D. K. Huntley (Alexandria, Va.: American Counseling Association, 1995), 59.

11. "Born Again Christians Just As Likely to Divorce As Are Non-Christians" (September 8, 2004), Barna Group, http://www.barna.org/barna-update/article/5-barna-update/194-born-again-christians-just-as-likely-to-divorce-as-are-non-christians. This is further substantiated in a more recent Barna report, "New Marriage and Divorce Statistics Released" (March 31, 2008), http://www.barna.org/barna-update/article/15-familykids/42-new-marriage-and-divorce-statistics-released.

12. James P. Bowers, "A Wesleyan-Pentecostal Approach to Christian Formation," *Journal of Pentecostal Theology* 3 (April 1995): 59. Bowers looks at the connection between a discipleship crisis and an identity crisis in the Pentecostal church. Numerous others in both Pentecostal and evangelical churches have called the present crisis a crisis of discipleship. Even the Willow Creek Association, which made the seeker-friendly model popular, has admitted a need to reassess their processes and the resulting disciples they are producing (see the article "Willow Creek Repents?" at http://www.outofur.com/archives/2007/10/willow_creek_re.html).

Chapter 3: Passing the Baton (Biblically Speaking)

1. Todd M. Johnson, David B. Barrett, and Peter F. Crossing, "Missiometrics 2008: Reality Checks for Christian World Communions," *International Bulletin of Missionary Research* 32, no. 1 (2008), 27–30. In a personal meeting in 2010, Todd Johnson estimated the number to stand around 640 million. In 2012, however, he adjusted this number to 614 million.

2. Philip Jenks, "Mainline Church Membership Decline Continues—but More Slowly" (February 14, 2011), Worldwide Faith News, http://archive.wfn.org/2011/02/msg00045.html. The National Council of Churches annual membership study revealed that mainline denominations were continuing to decline while Pentecostal denominations like the Assemblies of God and the Church of God were increasing in America. Church historian Vinson Synan believes that the Assemblies of God will be the largest denomination in the world within a few years.

3. Philip Jenkins, *The Next Christendom: The Coming of Global Christianity* (Oxford: Oxford University Press, 2007), 160. Jenkins charts a shift in Christianity from the west to the east and from the north to the south that is taking place in the twenty-first century. These are only some of the transitions the Church is presently enduring. Other shifts include methodological shifts, denominational shifts and generational shifts.

4. William M. Wilson and Mary Banks, *Empowered21 Conversation Process Executive Summary* (Cleveland, Tenn.: International Center for Spiritual Renewal, 2010).

5. Ibid., 5–6. Eight major conversation themes informed the Congress and formed major areas of need to be addressed by the Spirit-empowered movement in the twenty-first century.

6. Ibid. Four different meetings with groups of students at Oral Roberts University took place over three semesters from the spring of 2009 through the spring of 2010. The groups included student government officers, floor chaplains and selected spiritual leaders from campus.

7. Rickie D. Moore, "The Prophet as Mentor: A Crucial Facet of the Biblical Presentations of Moses, Elijah, and Isaiah," *Journal of Pentecostal Theology* 15 (2007): 160.

8. D. W. Slocumb, "Priorities and Hope for Non-Traditional Families from the Book of Ruth" (lecture, Pentecostal Theological Seminary, Cleveland, Tenn., June 15, 2011). Slocumb considers the book of Ruth as an account of hope for nontraditional families. Certainly the situation of this mother-in-law and daughter-in-law was one of overcoming the odds. The intergenerational connection is critical to understanding the blessings of the book of Ruth and how Boaz becomes part of the lineage of David and thus of Jesus Christ (Ruth 4:21–22).

9. Care should be taken, however, to separate the common Christian practice of discipleship from aberrations of mentoring in Greek society, such as pederasty. See Nicole Holmen, "Examining Greek Pederastic Relationships," *Student Pulse Academic Journal* 2, no. 2 (2010), http://www.studentpulse.com/articles/175/examining-greek-pederastic-relationships. Holmen discusses this practice, in which an older man would mentor a younger man with sexual practices involved. This perverted practice was justified by its enthusiasts using the mentoring overtone, while at the center of the relationship was actually homosexual practice with a young teenage boy. This practice was common and idealized in Greek society, but it is still important in the twenty-first century context. The violation of the young by mentors continues to be problematic, as demonstrated by cases of abuse in the Catholic Church in which priests violated young men in mentoring relationships. It is perhaps also demonstrated in the charismatic church by the recent Eddie Long case in Atlanta. Certainly this perversion of intergenerational mentoring should be guarded against by establishing proper boundaries and controls in mentoring relationships.

Chapter 4: Generation to Generation

1. Peter Hammond, "Jonathan Edwards: A Mind on Fire for Christ" (accessed January 29, 2012), The Reformation Society, http://www.reformationsa.org/articles/Jonathan%20Edwards.htm.

Chapter 5: Spiritual Parents Needed Now!

1. "People and Society: World" (accessed March 23, 2012), Central Intelligence Agency, The World Factbook, https://www.cia.gov/library/publications/the-world-factbook/geos/xx.html.

2. "Major Religions of the World Ranked by Number of Adherents" (accessed March 23, 2012), Adherents.com, www.adherents.com/Religions_By_Adherents.html. See also "Major Religions of the World Ranked by Number of Adherents"

(accessed March 23, 2012), ChartsBin Statistics Collector Team 2009, http://chartsbin .com/view/3nr.

3. "People and Society: World" (accessed March 23, 2012), Central Intelligence Agency, The World Factbook, https://www.cia.gov/library/publications /the-world-factbook/geos/xx.html.

4. Matt Rosenberg, "Current World Population" (January 26, 2012), About .com Geography, http://geography.about.com/od/obtainpopulationdata/a/world population.htm.

Chapter 6: Sons and Daughters Wanted

1. William M. Wilson, *Providing a Measurable Intergenerational Retreat Model for Local Church Use in Addressing the Cry of New Generations for Spiritual Fathers and Mothers* (Cleveland, Tenn.: International Center for Spiritual Renewal, 2010), Appendix A.

2. Robin Marantz Henig, "What Is It About 20-Somethings?" (August 18, 2010), *The New York Times Sunday Magazine*, http://www.nytimes.com/2010/08/22 /magazine/22Adulthood-t.html?pagewanted=all.

3. Ibid.

4. Ibid.

Chapter 8: Releasing the Spirit of Adoption

1. William M. Wilson, *Providing a Measurable Intergenerational Retreat Model for Local Church Use in Addressing the Cry of New Generations for Spiritual Fathers and Mothers* (Cleveland, Tenn.: International Center for Spiritual Renewal, 2010), Appendix A.

2. "Abortion Statistics: United States Data and Trends" (accessed April 9, 2012), National Right to Life Committee, http://www.nrlc.org/Factsheets/FS03 _AbortionInTheUS.pdf.

3. Ibid.

4. "Adoption Factbook Reveals New Domestic Adoption Study; Leads Discussion on Current State of Adoption" (May 24, 2011), National Council for Adoption, http://www.adoptioncouncil.org/images/stories/Adoption_Factbook_Press _Release_Extended.pdf.

5. Ellen Hermon, "Adoption Statistics" (accessed April 9, 2012), The Adoption History Project, http://darkwing.uoregon.edu/~adoption/topics/adoptionstatistics.htm.

6. "Facts: Young People" (accessed April 9, 2012), World Population Foundation, http://www.wpf.org/reproductive_rights_article/facts.

7. "Testimony of John Carro" (April 16, 1964), The Kennedy Assassination, http://mcadams.posc.mu.edu/russ/testimony/carro.htm.

Chapter 10: A Father's Love

1. "Fatherly Love," *Positive Living*, September/October 1995, 15. Cited in *In Other Words . . . The Christian Communicator's Research* 8, no. 2 (spring 1998): 8.

William (Billy) M. Wilson currently serves as executive director of the International Center for Spiritual Renewal, whose mission is to help restore spiritual integrity, promote scriptural unity and encourage social responsibility in the Body of Christ.

In 2006 the Center for Spiritual Renewal and Dr. Wilson provided leadership for the Azusa Street Centennial, the 100-year celebration of the Azusa Street revival. More than 50,000 people from 114 nations met in Los Angeles, California, for the weeklong event.

The Center for Spiritual Renewal presently facilitates Empowered21, a global initiative among Spirit-empowered denominations, ministries and churches designed to help shape the future of the fastest-growing Christian movement in the history of the world. Serving as chair and executive director of Empowered21 since its inception in 2008, Billy successfully guided 17 unique conversations on 5 continents, culminating in a global congress in April 2010 with 10,000 attendees from 96 nations meeting on the campus of Oral Roberts University in Tulsa, Oklahoma. Following the congress, Empowered21 has grown rapidly around the world, with 11 regional leadership cabinets established on 6 different continents that work together by focusing on critical issues and connecting generations for intergenerational blessing and impartation. Wilson also serves as co-chair of the Empowered21 Global Council with Pastor Jack Hayford.

Billy is executive producer and host of Voice of Salvation Ministries' *World Impact with Billy Wilson*. This weekly television program can now be seen in more than 150 nations with a potential viewing audience of 500 million people. Wilson chairs the executive cabinet of the Awakening America Alliance, an initiative of the International Center for Spiritual Renewal with the goal of uniting evangelical, Pentecostal and charismatic movements for an increased awareness of the deep spiritual need in modern America and for pursuit of a new Christ awakening in the United States. He also serves on numerous boards and committees, including the Oral Roberts University board of trustees, the Mission America Coalition (Lausanne Movement U.S.A.) facilitation committee, the Pentecostal World Fellowship advisory board and the International Christian Embassy Jerusalem advisory committee.

During more than 32 years of ministry, Wilson has served as church administrator, international youth director, senior pastor and international evangelist, personally ministering in more than 80 nations. He has authored numerous articles, sermon series, video projects and books, including *Fasting Forward: Advancing Your Spiritual Life Through Fasting, Marriage Recovery: The A to Z Guide to Reconciliation, God's A to Z Guide to Sexual Intimacy in Marriage, The Parenthood Plan: God's A to Z for Successful Parenting* and *Foundations of Faith*. Dr. Wilson holds a bachelor of science degree from Western Kentucky University, a master of arts from Church of God Theological Seminary and a doctor of ministry from Pentecostal Theological Seminary.

Billy and his wife, Lisa, currently reside in Cleveland, Tennessee. They have one daughter, Sara, who presently serves as a missionary in Paraguay with her husband,

Shaun, and their children, Abigail and Samuel. The Wilsons' son, Ashley, is currently pastoring a new church plant in Lexington, Kentucky, along with his wife, Jamie, and their children, Anna, Aaron and Amelia.

To obtain further information on Billy's ministry and the initiatives he serves, please write, call or visit the following websites:

International Center for Spiritual Renewal
Empowered21
World Impact with Billy Wilson
P.O. Box 3986
Cleveland, TN 37320
(423) 478-7078
www.empowered21.org
www.worldimpact.tv
www.awakeningamerica.us